www.ChildCareExchange.com

Exchange™

The Early Childhood Leaders' Magazine Since 1978

Professionalism

A Beginnings Workshop Book

Edited by Bonnie Neugebauer

PROFESSIONALISM

A Beginnings Workshop Book

These articles were collected from the Beginnings Workshop feature of *Exchange —
The Early Childhood Leaders' Magazine*. Every attempt has been made to update information
on authors and other contributors to these articles. We apologize for any biographical
information that is not current.

Exchange is a bimonthly management magazine for directors and owners of early childhood
programs. For more information about *Exchange* and other Exchange publications for
directors and teachers, contact:

Exchange
PO Box 3249
Redmond, WA 98073-3249
(800) 221-2864
www.ChildCareExchange.com

ISBN 978-0-942702-41-5

Printed in the United States of America

© Exchange Press, Inc., 2008

Cover Photograph by Nancy Lessard

PROFESSIONALISM

A Beginnings Workshop Book

MENTORING

OBSERVING CHILDREN

COLLABORATION

CHILD CARE IN UNIQUE ENVIRONMENTS

Being Teachers

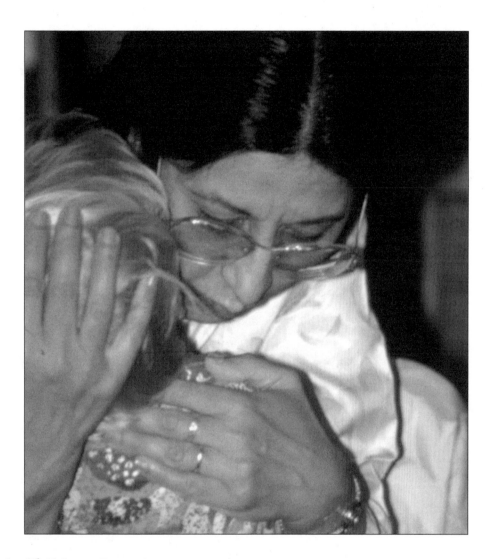

BEING TEACHERS

The Elephant's Child as Caregiver

by Elizabeth Jones

. . . But there was one Elephant —
a new Elephant —
an Elephant's Child —
who was full of 'satiable curtiosity,
and that means he asked ever so many questions. . . .

— Rudyard Kipling, *The Elephant's Child*

Do you ask questions? Young children do, as you've no doubt noticed. The Elephant's Child asked questions about everything he saw, or heard, or felt, or smelt, and so do they. Young children's curiosity, though sometimes exhausting for adults, is part of their charm. The world is a new place for them, and they want to know everything about it.

Do you? Or have you learned better, over years of schooling and being properly brought up? *What you don't know won't hurt you* is part of our folk wisdom. Don't ask questions and you won't get in trouble.

I think young children provide us with good models for our own learning. Being an active learner is a way to *stay interested* — in one's job, one's relationships, one's life. And it's a way to gain some power, to be able to predict and control some of the things that go on in our lives. *Knowledge gives power* is another, contradictory, part of our folk wisdom.

What's the worst thing that can happen to you if you're curious, if you observe carefully, if you ask, "Why?" You might get scolded or told it's none of your business. You might put someone else on the defensive. It helps to learn to time your questions and to ask them respectfully, with care for the feelings of others. But you might, on the other hand, learn some new and useful things. Make some deeper friendships. Become a more competent caregiver. I think it's worth the risk, and so I'd like to suggest some ways for teachers at work to be curious just like the Elephant's Child.

Being curious about children

What makes children tick? Why do they behave as they do? What are they thinking? Feeling? How can you find out? Observing children to try to understand their behavior is a basic competence for caregivers. Children learn through play; and their play serves as a clue to what's important to them, what they're trying to figure out and master. Programs that provide ample opportunity for children to play simultaneously provide opportunity for adults to learn by child watching. When play is going well, you're free to observe, to focus on the questions you have about the children.

Jamie's sitting in the sandbox all by herself. She looks very serious, but not sad, as she lets the sand dribble through her fingers again and again. Now she's picked up a shovel and is starting to dig a hole — just a little one. Is Jamie okay? She's new to the center and hasn't played with other children yet. Is the sand a good place for her to begin feeling at home?

Did Maya bite David again? David's mom is going to be so mad. She thinks we should kick Maya out of child care. What can you do with a two year old biter? Maya never seems mad when she bites — is she just trying to play with David? But you can't play with your teeth. . . . How come Lucy's afraid to climb the jungle gym? Are there other things she's afraid of? When does Jacob suck his thumb and when doesn't he? Is it possible to find him more experiences which make him confident?

You might get some answers by asking a child directly: "Why do you like to bring your teddy to school?" "Is your mom back from her trip yet?" You'll get more answers by observing behavior and making guesses about the reasons for it. In making guesses, you keep trying to put yourself in the child's shoes, to understand what the world looks and feels like at three years old. You work at getting back in touch with your own feelings and confusions and joys as a young child. And because you were only one child, you try to get in touch with other adults' childhood experiences which may have been different from your own. You may find out more about colleagues' experiences as you talk together about problems you're having with a child:

"Hey, what's going on with Paul?" "He's really been crying a lot lately. He won't talk about it." "I tried to talk to his mom, but she's under a lot of stress." "Last year when Paul was in my class, we went through a period like this, and I tried. . . ." "I tried that but it didn't seem to work." "Maybe if you. . . ." "You know, crying kids really get on my nerves, and I think that's why I'm not dealing with this so well." "Oh, crying I can handle, it's the whining that's tough for me." "My mom used to slap me if I whined. But my grandma just took me on her lap. . . ."

Being curious about colleagues

Do you like the other people you work with? Do you trust them to care about the children and the program, to do good things for children? Do you trust them to care about you? How well do you know them? Would you like to know them better?

I had to leave the center to pick up my daughter when she got sick at school, and Carrie volunteered to work the rest of my shift, just like that. She'd been on since 7:00 and she was tired, yet she said "Go ahead, I'll stay" without thinking twice about it. That really made me feel cared for. I'll help her out next time — or someone else who needs it.

We were all so excited when Ellen finally got pregnant; it was like we were her family. The kids, too — it was really celebration time for all of us.

A director I know took over a program which wasn't a very good one for either children or adults. She didn't think the adults were being very responsible with children — but instead of just criticizing them, she tried to find ways to meet their needs. To do that, she had to get curious about them as people. She wrote to me about it:

I sincerely believe that only when individuals feel that they are important and cared about, and only when their needs are being met, are they capable of doing the same for others. My role as an administrator to a great extent has been to try to get to know what the needs of my staff are.

I have spent a great deal of time listening and encouraging and defending each and every staff member. I have tried to

say nothing so that individuals could find out for themselves.

Because we are all fallible, we are still struggling together. But we are all trying to be more humane with one another, and perhaps some day our program will be one in which there is room for everyone to grow. (Morgan, 1980, pp. 46-47)

A year and a half later, she wrote:

We really have become a community of people caring about each other. There is space for people to be themselves and yet there is also room for real emotions and honest conflicts.

For people to grow I think you have to create a climate of trust. Each of us can change only when we open ourselves up to possibilities, and we can do that only when we feel safe and accepted. I was able to gain trust by focusing on people's strengths instead of their weaknesses, and by giving adult needs priority.

Because they had the time to get to know one another in a context other than with children (workshops, rap sessions, staff meetings, coffee klatching, etc.), and because they did not need to compete to prove their worth, they were able to relax and find out that they had more in common than they thought. We have come to see each other as real people with faults and virtues. (pp. 103-104)

To "find out that they had more in common than they thought" happens only when there is both curiosity and opportunity to talk and ask questions and share experiences. Most of us are most comfortable with people who are a lot like us — who share similar backgrounds and hold the same assumptions we do about the world.

In a group in which there are many or large differences among people, we have to keep problem solving — learning about each other. Diversity guarantees the constant recurrence of the unexpected. A homogeneous group is tidier, but boring; it leads to smugness on everyone's part. No one questions each other's assumptions (except, of course, the children, who are good at that sort of thing).

Maria and Lupe are cousins. They took care of each other's kids, growing up; now, both grandmas, they still like taking care, and so they work at the center. They love brushing hair and tying bows and serving lunch to the kids. They're really uneasy with the new aide, Joshua, who's 20 years old and a college dropout. His beard is scruffy and he roughhouses with the kids, and he let them get their shoes wet in the puddles yesterday. What kind of caregiving is that?

I find that having my assumptions questioned is exceedingly good for me. It shakes up my patterns of thinking and forces me to reexamine them. Increasingly I have come to believe that the *unexpected* question or comment, which is a product either of diversity or of divergent thinking, has exceptional educational value. The little boy in the fairy tale who asked why the emperor had no clothes on provides a nice example. Children often notice the discrepancies in our world and comment on them. We can dismiss them as just children in an effort to keep our dignity and prejudices intact.

But dignity gets in the way of understanding. Working hard to maintain our image as persons worthy of respect, we lose the opportunity of seeing the world freshly. Learning about children is a chance to reexamine our adult assumptions. Learning about each other is a chance to reexamine our assumptions about caregivers — who's a good one, and why aren't you like me? Decentering — getting past using myself as the model for how everyone else ought to be — is a lifelong struggle for me. I find I can begin to do it by asking other people questions to which I really want to know the answer — unloaded questions, asked out of curiosity rather than as veiled criticism. That's hard to do, but I get better with practice. If veiled complaints are the rule where you work, changing expectations will take awhile.

Question asking might go something like this:

The director and three caregivers are having coffee during nap time. Pam and Debby, in the three year old room, had a fairly disastrous experience when they brought a new water table into the room yesterday. All the children wanted to play there at once. Jason poured a whole pitcher of water on the floor, Cindy slipped in it, and Charley stepped on her finger while she screamed and screamed. It was one of those days.

Pam is still angry. The water table was Debby's idea, backed up by the director, and Pam had her doubts from the beginning. She doesn't approve of messy activities. "Why did you want to have a water table anyway?" is her first question.

"Do you really want to know the answer, Pam, or are you just mad at Debby?" the director asks.

"I'm mad, and she's already explained it to me — but, yes, I think I do want to hear her reasons again."

Debby repeats them. "Children need sensory experience, and it's been a long winter, and they've had no water play outside. They can learn pouring skills which are useful at snack time. Water relaxes children. . . ."

"They were not relaxed! They were hyper, and so was I!" breaks in Pam. Debby starts to cry. She hates being yelled at. Pam apologizes for making her cry, and the thread is getting lost.

"Could one of you try another question?" asks the director. "Does either of you want to know why Jason poured the water on the floor?"

"Yes, I do," sniffled Debby. "Pam, why did he?"

"He was mad, I think," says Pam. "Charley was trying to grab the pitcher from Jason, and I think he intended to pour the water on Charley."

"I have a question," says the teacher of the fours. "How many pitchers were available? And how many kids were at the water table?"

"One — and 13," says Debby. "Oh — I didn't plan very well, did I?"

It may or may not be relevant to this particular dispute that Pam is black and middle aged and Debby is young and white and a recent college graduate in early childhood education. When people are different from each other in culture, age, values, and experiences, the possibilities for misunderstanding escalate.

Some people yell at children; some people don't. Some people hug children a lot; others don't. Some people put on four year olds' clothes for them; others expect four year olds to put on their own clothes, even if it's less efficient. Some of these differences reflect personal idiosyncrasies, some reflect professional training, some reflect basic cultural differences. All of them can cause frustration.

Curiosity can be an effective way of moving past frustration. If I can get interested in why you do what you do, instead of just mad at you because you don't do it my way, both of us will expand our base of understanding of human behavior.

Being curious about your director

Your director is one of your colleagues, too; and if she's been a teacher or caregiver, she probably has some good stories to tell about her experiences with children. You might want to invite her to if she doesn't do it spontaneously. She's had dilemmas and successes and failures, too; she probably knows something about problem solving. Especially if you're new on the job, give her a chance to teach you something — even if you're someone with a lot of experience in other programs. She may need to assert her authority, to make sure you understand and appreciate *this* program. If you say, out loud or in your head, "Well, that isn't the way we did it on my last job," you're cutting off your chance to learn some new ways. Try curiosity as a strategy; what is there to be learned here?

As one director describes it: "Different people need differing amounts and kinds of structure and support. There are some people who, because of their experience and competence, I am going to trust a whole lot; I won't give them as much direction."

With Nancy, who has been at the center for awhile and is full of good ideas, this director provides very informal supervision — a casual "How's it going?" or "What's happening this week?" and an open door when Nancy wants to talk. Nancy, for her part, makes a point of sending a child to the office with fresh-baked cookies from her class, mentioning a good book she's discovered, and chatting with the director about individual children and their growth.

Would you like to have that kind of trust? How do you get what you want from people who have authority over you? Basically, by making their jobs easier, not harder. What does your director like to do and not like to do? What especially bugs her? What can you find to like about her? What basis do you have for building a relationship? This doesn't imply that you're trying to be her *pet*; it simply recognizes that being in charge is a lonely role, and she's likely to appreciate you if you treat her as a human being doing a tough job.

Some people have an automatic anti-authority reaction: if you're my boss, I know you're not on my side. If you feel that way a lot, you're less likely to elicit trust from a director; you're more likely to be treated like a rebellious child. One director (Jambor, 1983) has written about her own frustrations in being expected to be *mom* by her staff — always there, always taking care of everyone. Do you expect that of yours? (Some directors, of course, probably are happiest as *mom* or *dad*.)

Being curious about yourself

Who are you? What do you care about? Why are you here? What interests you about children? What gives you pleasure in being with them? Which of your interests do you enjoy sharing with them? What are your goals for them?

Does all this seem obvious? Of course you know about yourself. In fact, most of us keep growing in self-understanding, and we learn in the same way we learn about other people — by observing and reflecting on our observations. Why did I get so mad when Marta dropped a cup yesterday? It was an accident. Did it trigger something from my own past that had very little to do with the present situation? Why do I find it so hard to like Jorge? I catch myself being almost mean to him — sarcastic, in a way that just isn't appropriate with little kids. Why do I do that?

Sometimes a friend or colleague can help us think through our self-observations if we're willing to share them. It can be uncomfortable, learning more about ourselves, especially about the parts of ourselves we really don't like. Some people go to therapists to get help with this process, to have someone who can listen thoughtfully to their questions about themselves.

What do you like to do with children? Sing, cook, go on walks, pet animals, have conversations, watch them playing, snuggle,

Curiosity as Play

Children become active learners through play. So do adults. Play is making choices and exploring possibilities, at any age. It's being alive and interested, curious and innovative.

The average life of a child care worker isn't very long. Every year or so, many of them leave. That's not good for the children in their care who were just getting attached to them. But it's unavoidable, isn't it, given the low pay and high demands of caregiving? Why, then, do some centers, with no better pay, seem to keep their staffs much longer than others? People stick around when they like the work — when they believe it's important and when it's satisfying on a day-to-day basis.

Try this idea. Adults, like children, need to play. What are the legitimate ways in which caregivers can play on the job? Here are some I've observed:

■ Moving furniture.

■ Creating bulletin boards and displays.

■ Making things for children's use.

■ Playing with materials with children.

■ Kidding, telling jokes, playing silly games, laughing.

■ Socializing with other adults.

■ Going places.

■ Being entertained.

■ Cuddling children.

■ Creating celebrations for children and for staff.

■ Arguing with other adults (a form of drama).

■ Intellectual challenges. Can I figure out this child's behavior? Can I organize the space so it will work better?

■ Spontaneous invention.

■ Doing, and being acknowledged for, things that you do well.

■ Taking *well days*.

Some of these ways to play generate new learning. Others may not — but all may contribute to burnout avoidance.

comb hair, and wash faces? Do you get to do what you like to do on your job? If not, could you? If you're a caregiver spending every day with children, it's important that you have many opportunities to be a decision maker, to say, "This is what I want to do next." Not at the children's expense, but in response to both your needs and theirs. If caregivers are contented and growing, children are more likely to be contented and growing, too.

Which describes you better: You like parenting children; you like teaching children; you like playing with children? Competence in child care may be based on any of these enjoyments. Parenting is being responsible, taking good care of children, appreciating their growth; if you're experienced as a parent, that may be the role you fall into naturally in child care. Teaching implies particular interest in children's thinking and problem solving, in what they know and understand — and in helping them learn. Playing with children implies being in touch with the child in yourself.

What kind of learner are you? How do you learn best? Different people learn by reading, by taking classes, by observing children's behavior, by discussing their experiences with colleagues and friends, by going to conferences and workshops, by trying things for themselves and seeing what happens.

Which of these things work for you? Does your center encourage you to keep learning and give you credit for what you do?

A child care center is a *living place* for children and adults. It should be a good place to live together and learn together about the world. What are you learning at your work? What risks are you taking?

Learning and risk taking go together. That curious Elephant's Child happened to want to know what the Crocodile had for dinner, and when he went off to the river to find out, he very nearly *was* the Crocodile's dinner. He needed help to get loose, and in the process his little nose got stretched into "a really truly trunk, same as all elephants have today." It hurt, getting stretched. But it proved to be very useful for the rest of his life.

References

Jambor, N. (1983). "The Administrator as Mom." In Sharon Stine (editor), *Administration: A Bedside Guide*. Pasadena, CA: Pacific Oaks.

Morgan, C. (1983). "Journal of a Day Care Administrator." Pacific Oaks College master's project, 1980. Adapted in Sharon Stine (editor), *Administration: A Bedside Guide*. Pasadena, CA: Pacific Oaks.

Elizabeth Jones has been a member of the Human Development faculty at Pacific Oaks College in Pasadena, California, for many years. When she was little, her mother read her *The Elephant's Child*, and she is still "full of 'satiable curiosity" about learners of all ages and the experiences that enable them to grow. Her most recent curiosities can be found in *Playing to Get Smart* (2006, Teachers College) and *Teaching Adults Revisited* (in press 2007, NAEYC).

BEING TEACHERS

Teachers and Then Some: Profiles of Three Teachers

based on interviews with Carol Hillman, Alex Pirie, and Carolee Fucigna

Each of the three teachers here are inventors — they have discovered ways to combine their teaching of young children with very deep and long-lasting aspects of their lives as active, questioning adults.

Carol Hillman: Gardener, naturalist, teacher

I believe deeply that what you are outside of school affects what you are in school. I have a farm in Massachusetts that has for many years been a resource to me and to the children in my classroom.

There I grow things, looking after the whole process myself. I like having the knowledge that I can grow vegetables or flowers without relying on chemicals. The flowers are just as important as the edible things. I pick and dry many of them, making everlasting bouquets from them. The whole process gives me a feeling of self-sufficiency and a kind of calmness.

Those feelings translate to the classroom in ways that you might not suspect. I come to the classroom with a keen sense of the pleasure it can be to do with what you have, without having to go out and buy things. I try to show the children those same pleasures. We make bird feeders from cups and chenille-wrapped wire. They take the feeders home and have a season's worth of birds coming and going. For me, that is much better than robots or superheroes.

Growing things take attention — you are constantly watching what needs water, what needs thinning, what can be picked. I want to communicate that awareness to children. Every morning we have a meeting, and I ask them what they notice that is different. Almost every day we go outdoors, not just to a playground, but to the woods that surround us on practically all

sides. I want the children to become investigators in the natural world: I want them to be curious about the stream, the trees, and the leaves on the ground.

Something else is fed by growing things — my aesthetic sense, a love for beautiful arrangements, shapes, and colors. Many years ago, on my first job after college, I worked at an art gallery in New York City and learned, among other things, how to hang an exhibition. Since then, I have carried with me the importance of placement, whether I am placing blocks on a shelf or plants in a garden.

That, too, carries over to the classroom. The blocks, the baskets of parquetry blocks, the puzzles and pegboards must each stand apart to command their own space and importance. What I am after is a sense of order, not a strict cleanliness — children need messiness, too.

But beyond that sense of order, my experiences in gardens and the wider outdoors have given me a taste for naturally beautiful things. Rather than stickers or predrawn forms, the children in my classes make collages from shells and sand, sweet gum pods, acorns, and pine cones.

Outside my garden, an important part of my life as a part-time naturalist is raising monarch butterflies. For a number of years, I've worked with Dr. Fred Urquart of Toronto, who was trying to locate the hidden spot where monarchs migrate during the winter months. I've been a part of that search by raising, tagging, and releasing butterflies. After a lifetime of tracking the butterflies marked by many people such as myself, Urquart was able to locate the monarch's wintering spot high in the mountains near Mexico City.

I have a whole portion of my garden devoted to milkweed, which is the sole food source for monarchs. I find the small caterpillars on the plants and take them into school. During the first few weeks of school each year, the children and I watch the whole metamorphosis — from caterpillar, through chrysalis, to butterfly. We keep the monarchs in a huge butterfly case for a few days after they emerge. Then, on warm, blue sky days, children take turns holding and releasing the monarchs into the air. It is probably a moment they won't forget.

Alex Pirie:
Teacher, woodworker, castle builder

I found my way into teaching by a fluke. I was involved in organizing a labor union at Channel 2, where I was the foreman in the scene shop. When we lost the first vote, I realized I was burned out by all the organizing that had been involved and didn't see much future in the work without a union.

At the school where my daughter was, there had been a woodworking program ever since the 1940s. I heard about a part-time position and thought there might be something for me in teaching what I knew about wood and carpentry, so I began working with fourth through sixth graders. In two years, I had shifted over to being the full-time woodworking teacher for kindergarten through sixth grades.

After four to five years, I became a single parent and had to decide how to cut my job time back. I was drawn to staying with the younger children. With them, there was less pressure to teach *craft*, no pressure to teach them to make joints or to sand properly, and the freedom to let them determine how they would use the class. The school would also let me work with them in small groups.

That freedom was important to me. I had always thought long and hard about what I wanted in my daughter's education. I had been a producer of "Twenty-One Inch Classroom," an educational television program, and had become disillusioned with that. I had been doing a great deal of reading of A. S. Neill. In the woodworking shop with four year olds, I was free to invent my own 45 minute version of what I believed in. I might be building a boat with a child; but we could talk about measuring, or words, or being afraid of the ocean. We can slave over getting the edges to join, or we could just paint in the details.

I don't know if wood is any better than clay or drawing for young children, but it is a wonderful material. It allows you ways to work with all kinds of different learning styles. You can plan and assemble a construction or you can remove pieces like a sculptor. That means you can either build your way towards something or you can *see into the wood* and try to bring that something out. You can just slam and bang an alligator together, or you can work on it forever, cutting the shapes, using the grain. You can leave the wood plain, just letting it speak for itself, or you can really deck it out with paint, pasted-on cloth, and sparkles.

Some people think of wood as bulky and demanding and not likely to give a child much chance for expression. But I can tell you that's not the case. I worked with a child whose mother had cancer. The child was nervous and stressed. Her family was walking that fine line between being honest and trying not to scare the child. In woodworking, she spent a lot of time making germs. She used that process to think through a whole set of questions about living and dying and contagion. When she was done, she had a concrete object that she could use with me to play out other questions or fears.

My original hunches about working with younger children have been right. If you have four children at a time, you can be a participant teacher — you can pay intense attention to each one of those children. I have this image of myself as being like the rotor in the distributor of a motor. That's the part that drops current to each of the spark plugs. That's me — I just keep revolving from child to child — sparking them.

It has also turned out to be a place where I can make good use of the whole patchwork of my work experiences. Since I didn't come out of teacher training, I was totally open; I had very few ideas about what had to be accomplished and in what order. That left me free to stop teaching my *subject* whenever I saw some larger need. Once, in the middle of a class of fifth graders, I heard myself saying, "We're not going to do shop right now, we're going to talk about a problem of scapegoating that is going on."

Also, being a woodworker and a television producer, I didn't have fixed ideas about what children of a certain age can and can't do. So I began to let the four year olds learn to use crosscut saws — not without watching them, but by relying on their own natural skills and caution. They were, and are, wonderful teachers.

In the late '70s, my woodworking with children took on a new dimension. I am one of those people that if I had a giant attic it would be bursting at the seams. I just couldn't stand letting all those little rounds from birdhouse windows and all those cuts from boat bows hit the trash. I had to save them. As the pile mounted, I had to find a way to use them, so I built a very crude castle by gluing them together. I painted it and gave it to the school auction. But that wasn't the end of my compulsion.

Over the last six years, I have been building more and more elaborate castles with those bits — I suppose, in part, because they give a voice to the creative, artistic side of me. I work right there in the shop, building on my break or on weekends. As a result, the children can see my progress — or lack of it. One day, one of them will notice that the wall has been stuck at six inches for a couple of weeks, and we begin to talk about it. I am very open with them about how I sometimes get stuck or don't like what I'm doing. Sometimes they come in on Monday and see a castle has grown by leaps and bounds. Then we can talk about things like insight and inspiration.

Just having the castles in the middle of the studio has made the children aware of me as a worker. They ask what I do with the castles; and I explain that I sell them through a store, that the store takes 30%, and that I get the rest. I don't know what it is but many of them think of me as a parent, not as someone who works at and is paid for teaching.

The castles have provided a concrete way to talk about teachers as workers. They have also given me a chance to talk about not being just a teacher. Teaching is very important to me; it isn't something I want to give up. But it doesn't answer everything I have in me. There is an artist part that is always looking around for ways to be active. In the past years, the castles have been my way of cracking the ideas of specialization — the notion that I, or any other teacher, should be *all teacher*. I daydream about opening up that crack for the kindergarten teacher in my building who is a fine potter. In fact, my most grandiose daydream — I guess you could call it my biggest castle in the air — is to invent a way or a place for all teachers to act on their creativity.

Carolee Fucigna: Teacher and Rresearcher

Maybe research is in my blood. My father was a researcher, and I worked for him doing market research during my summers in college. While I was testing reflecting jackets for 3M, I can remember wishing that his company was more involved with children's issues.

When I left college, I started teaching toddlers at a child care center affiliated with Harvard. It wasn't long before I found myself using a voucher I had gotten for supervising a student teacher to take a course on research methods. One day in class the professor announced he was starting a new research project on children's drawing. I jumped at the chance — it was an opportunity to get off the sidelines, and I had always been fascinated by children's art work.

As a result of volunteering, I came to know a diverse group of people working in research on children's drawing in the Boston area. Through one of them, I became involved in a second research project, a long-term study of children's early symbolic development. For two years, I had the chance to formulate basic questions about how children learn to draw and to test my ideas by analyzing data.

But during that time, I realized that I missed working with young children. I searched for a graduate school, looking for a program which had both a strong research and a strong teaching component. I found that program at Tufts University, where I was both a masters candidate and a teacher of three and four year olds in the lab school, the Eliot-Pearson Children's School.

My thesis grew out of what I noticed about toddlers' earliest drawings. Most people think that two year olds only scribble. But I noticed that even though their slashes and dots hardly look like pictures, toddlers may be representing their experiences with marks. For instance, if you name the parts of a body, a toddler can make a mark at the top for a head and two marks at the bottom of the paper for legs. No one had ever systematically explored these very early origins of picturing. So that's what I set out to do.

Being a researcher changed my teaching. First of all, it taught me how to formulate questions and reflect on classroom issues. For example: for about a week, the children in my class were suddenly very involved in painting. But now I find that just the same four or five children paint each day. Now I have some tools to start asking questions: What's happened? Does it have to do with the set up of materials? Is there another compelling activity that is pulling children away from painting? Is there enough teacher attention paid to children when they paint? Once I've investigated these different possibilities, I get closer to finding out what action I can take to reinspire interest in painting.

Second, my stint as a researcher taught me to think developmentally. I now think about curriculum in terms of a sequence of activities. I am always asking myself, "What activity will build on earlier skills and add something new that will extend the children's learning?" For instance, once children have become skilled enough to experiment with painting expert lines, I decide to add a large brush to the easel to add to the small brush that has always been there. That way I am inviting them to extend their familiar knowledge of painting by exploring possible differences in line quality.

Third, as a researcher, I think I have gained a strong developmental knowledge of children. As a result, I can talk with them about what they are trying to accomplish. They know that I am tuned in to the issues that they are dealing with. So when I added that big brush, I was ready to look at children's paintings and say, "Hey, look at how much blue you can put on with that big brush. You've covered almost half your paper with blue and only had to put paint on your brush once."

Finally, I know that parents have an added respect for me, knowing that my work experience includes research. At parent conferences, I feel that they listen when I talk about the cognitive, as well as the expressive, goals of teaching art in the classroom.

It's important to acknowledge what being a researcher doesn't do for me as a teacher. It doesn't help me live with the consequences of the decisions I have to make. As a researcher, I could be perfectly satisfied with constructing a tidy theory. If it doesn't work out, that's part of the process. But the world of the classroom isn't tidy. A new brush will draw back some children, but not all. When I change one item, new issues crop up. Maybe the paper I've provided is too small for all these new broad strokes they're creating. In order to supply them with larger paper, I need a larger painting surface.

In a research project, you have the luxury of refining and refining a solution or answer to a problem; but in the classroom you have to move from problem to problem quickly because those problems are immediate and pressing. If I want to study the development of children's artistic skills as they unfold in the classroom, I am always balancing between my interest in reflecting on what is happening and my need to respond immediately to children's needs and behaviors.

What seems absolutely necessary — if I am going to be both teacher and researcher — is to have a supportive community of other teachers who believe in combining reflection and action. I need other teachers who are interested in going beyond the satisfaction of daily classroom interactions.

In addition, I need administrative support for my work. That means a director or a supervisor who will help me find funds for going to conferences and workshops, locate substitutes so that I can collect data from a small group of children, and also discuss ideas (or even the right statistical analyses).

People often suspect that research experience will draw teachers away from the classroom. That isn't the case for me. My teaching has left me much more invested in research questions that grow out of my life in the classroom. Right now, I want to understand more about children's fascination with superheroes, what makes children popular or unpopular, how to involve children in exploring representational work with clay and found materials. While research work has expanded and enriched my teaching, I also know that my classroom work has provided the most interesting problems to research.

BEING TEACHERS

Becoming Planners: Finding Time and Insight

based on an interview with Patricia Scallan-Berl

Ask any director, stop any teacher, and he will tell you that planning *makes the difference*. With time to plan, chaos can become calm, tension can give way to decent relations, seat-of-the-pants classroom management can become quality education. But I'd take those testimonies a step further. I'd claim that it's only when teachers become planners that teachers, as well as children, develop.

A skeptic might point out that teachers are already *developed* — after all, they're full-grown adults. But when I speak of teachers developing, I am not talking about them being just successful activity planners or classroom managers. I am thinking of teachers developing their teaching into an art, reflecting a deep sense of personal values and style — as a composer who writes good music or an author who crafts his individual story. Only if teachers are given the time to plan their work thoughtfully can they become artists in this sense.

Narrow versus broad planning

What you notice about novice teachers is that their plans are often narrow, short term, and teacher dependent. They plan just for specific activities. By comparison, skilled teachers plan for the long term, for broad objectives, and in terms of children's activities. Consider the simple example of teaching children the concept of a triangle. Inexperienced teachers may put in as much — or even more — preparation time as skilled teachers do. The new teacher may make a large poster with the word *triangle* in large colored letters. She may make sheets on which children are to color in triangles. She may provide an elastic cord so that children, working in threes, can make different triangle shapes at recess. But what she is creating is a set of activities about triangles, with no connection to children's earlier learning and no implications for what comes next. The next day it is on to squares and rectangles.

By comparison, skilled teachers plan in much more open and subtle ways. They start the year by setting up the block shelf so that the triangular shapes are in a different space from the cylinders and squares. Occasionally, they divide the block-building space into triangular wedges, rather than squares. They talk with children about how such working spaces turn out different structures. They make plans or photographs of the buildings children create. These records are placed in a book or a file that children turn to when they want ideas. When children paint wedges and pointed forms or build teepees or tents, experienced teachers talk about the *triangles* they have made. In other words, with skilled teachers, I am always aware of a *long arc* of planning. Those teachers are forever asking:

"Where might it go next?"

"What else might it connect to?"

It's conventional to think about the benefits of this kind of skilled planning for children — how it provides a richer classroom environment, a number of varied avenues for approaching basic concepts, developmentally sound sequences of learning. But I want to emphasize the benefits to teachers.

As they become skilled planners, teachers:

■ **Cease being at the mercy of the moment.** They learn how to build on what they have done earlier and how to make what they are doing now pay off in the future. This gives teachers a sense of accomplishment. When they overhear children talking about the triangle shapes they see in the trees outside, they can take pleasure in having laid the groundwork well.

■ **Buy time for reflection.** Skilled planning often involves making better use of what naturally occurs in the classroom (instead of scurrying to invent dittoes, cutouts, and teaching charts for every holiday and concept). In that way, skilled planning can actually free teachers from busy work and win them time to think about the *big* things they want to accomplish or change.

■ **Win the right to selection.** One of the byproducts of reflection is that teachers can begin to select the materials, the procedures, and the kinds of interactions that they believe in most deeply. Once teachers begin making choices based on their own experience and judgment, they are on their way to practicing teaching as an art.

Making planning possible

The question is, then, "How can schools create a climate in which teachers will be able to plan in these ways?" In my experience, there are a number of ways in which administrators and directors can create a climate in which teachers have the opportunity to plan:

■ **Planning for planning.** Good planning does not occur when wedged in at the end of a day or in occasional night meetings. School administrators must make *planning for planning* a part of their calendar. I have worked in centers and schools where we regularly found substitutes for teachers so that they could have an entire morning to lay out plans for the next semester. I have also been in a center where the school closed so that the teachers could work together for a full day. We had to plan for that day a year in advance. We wrote families a letter explaining our purpose and asking for their support. We even found college students willing to baby-sit in homes.

■ **Regularity.** Good planning can't take place in occasional blitzes. It is essential for every teacher to have at least 45 minutes a week to think ahead. The more responsible a teacher is, the more planning time he needs on a regular basis. I like to see my head teachers have as much as an hour and a half.

■ **Group work.** It isn't enough to plan alone. After all, teachers often work together in classroom teams, and each is also a contributing member of the center. Using whatever means are at my disposal, I find all my head teachers time to meet together at least four times a year. It is equally essential for the head teacher, assistants, and aides from any one classroom to have time to think ahead together.

Over the years, I have brought the teachers in my school together for an evening. After supper, we brainstorm possibilities for the coming year in small groups. Then we look over all the ideas, evaluating them. That way everyone, from head teachers to the newest aides, has a voice. Those hours are very

educational. Younger teachers see more experienced teachers modeling the kind of broad, subtle planning that comes with experience. Away from the demands of children and parents, teachers have the chance to talk through the issues of personal style and values that are at the heart of artful teaching.

■ **Resources.** Teachers' ability to plan develops with experience and the opportunity to observe skilled practitioners. But time is expensive, so it makes good sense to help the learning process along. For instance, teachers can:

— team up with still more experienced teachers (from their own or other centers) particularly when planning for extending or changing aspects of the curriculum.

— visit other schools and centers to find out how that staff finds time to plan, what they plan, who works together in planning.

— make use of courses at local colleges and universities. Teachers should explore the possibilities, talk with other people who have studied there, find instructors who are especially skilled at helping teachers gain insight into the goals they want to achieve and the way to pursue those goals.

Living out those plans

It is one thing to plan, another thing to live by those plans. Based on what I have seen, there are not one but three secret ingredients: cooperation, evaluation, and flexibility.

■ **Cooperation.** When it involves two or more teachers working together in classrooms, planning can be as complicated as working together in a marriage. It is particularly demanding when teachers have different personalities or philosophies: when one is assertive and the other is quiet or when one believes in strict instruction and the other supports a play-centered curriculum. It is critical that everyone put their cards on the table and participate in planning, rather than abdicate or sulk. Sometimes it is important for a director or a more experienced teacher to sit in. It can be that person's role to encourage everyone to put out ideas, to evaluate suggestions fairly, and to compromise.

■ **Evaluation.** Just because plans are laid doesn't mean they should unfold willy-nilly. Instead, teachers should engage in a cycle of planning-implementing-evaluating. Suppose two preschool teachers have a population of children with poor language skills. They might plan trips to the library, visits from an actor for a children's theater company, the purchase of a new set of puppets. But once these changes are underway, it is essential to take a long, hard look at whether what was planned is working. The teachers might find that all the coming and going and the novel equipment created more uproar than language development. By talking with other teachers working with similar children, they might learn that more concentrated in-class conversations and reading periods might be more effective. At that point, it is important to lay new plans, to try them out, and to evaluate again.

■ **Flexibility.** I stand behind my idea of ensuring that teachers have significant blocks of time released for planning. All the same, there is nothing wrong with seizing the odd moment. Teachers can arrive 15 minutes early, use nap time or playground time, grab the 10 minutes they spend straightening up the room to chat about a favorite long-term goal. The point is to keep the planning spark alive.

Patricia Scallan-Berl is a division vice president of mid-Atlantic operations for Bright Horizons Family Solutions. She is known nationally as a conference presenter and author of articles in child care center management and supervision. She has been a regular contributor to *Exchange* since 1978. In addition to her lovely family, Patricia has a passion for orchids, Springer Spaniels, and travel.

BEING TEACHERS

Backing Away Helpfully: Some Roles Teachers Shouldn't Fill

based on an interview with Penny Hauser-Cram

I suspect that if you asked for a definition of a good teacher most families would describe a cross between a chameleon and Wonderwoman — someone who is part developmental scholar, pediatrician, artist, and therapist, with a little bit of toy designer, janitor, and athlete mixed in. But based on my years as a teacher and a director, I have come to believe that there are at least some roles that teachers can't and shouldn't fill. Two roles that I have seen cause tension and hard feelings come immediately to mind: the role of family therapist and the role of parenting expert.

Parents need and want other adults in each of these roles. Since teachers and parents share an intimate, ongoing relationship centered on children they both care about, it is tempting for all sides to move from educational and developmental issues to personal, and even therapeutic, ones. A big challenge for teachers is to help parents find the help they need, without adopting those helping roles themselves.

Sharing children's development

Parents and teachers really do share children. Together they are involved in seeing one and sometimes several children through some of the largest developmental events of the early years: the transition from the home to school or a center, the process of making friends, the joys and struggles of learning to talk or even to begin reading. Because of daily involvement with a child, a teacher is often the first outsider to know the in's and out's of a family's workings: whether they ignore or attend to a child's illness; when they have had periods of disorganization; how they handle the stresses of being late, bathroom accidents, or a missing favorite book or toy. A teacher also learns a great deal of very revealing information about individual children: how late or early a baby sits up, walks, says a first word; how shy or aggressive a three year old is; how challenging or cooperative a four year old may be. Unlike friends or neighbors, who may have similar insights, teachers are in a position to evaluate —

they can compare a family or a child to many others they know.

A charged situation

Since parents are often deeply invested in how their children are developing, their discussions with teachers are often charged with emotion. Some parents resent or distrust teachers, particularly in cases where teachers and family members see the child or the purposes of early education differently. For example, imagine what happens when a father sees a boy as *active* and a teacher sees that child as *aggressive,* or when a mother wants her three year old to practice number facts and a teacher insists blocks and beads provide the *right* kinds of early mathematical experiences.

Other parents react to a teacher's knowledge by thinking: "Here is someone who already knows and cares about us. At last, here is someone I can really talk to." Then, when a teacher asks a question in a conference related to a child's life at home, the parent may see it as an invitation to go far beyond issues of the child's behavior or schooling. Suddenly, the teacher is catapulted into the role of a therapist or expert.

Spotting difficult situations

Sometimes teachers can anticipate that parents may desire additional advice, especially when a child's behavior has undergone a dramatic change. Discussing that change with parents is an important part of a teacher's responsibility, but such discussions can sometimes lead to areas beyond the scope and expertise of the teacher.

Imagine that during a conference a teacher says: "I have been wondering about Michael. The last two weeks he hasn't been playing with friends. He seems listless and tired. Has he been sleeping well?" The parent comes back with: "You're right. I'm glad you mentioned it. Things have been tough . . . there have been a lot of fights at night. We're thinking about separating, and I'm worried about Michael. What should I do?" Without meaning to, the teacher touched a nerve. The parent responded with a flood of intimate information and a request for help. Within a few moments, a teacher has become a parent's counselor.

A different type of difficult situation sometimes occurs when mother and father come to a conference with different points of view. Before the teacher can say much, it is clear that they see their child quite differently. One insists: "Shelley is a cry baby." The other interrupts: "She is not. She is just more sensitive than other children." Both turn to the teacher for confirmation. Suddenly, the teacher is playing the part of an arbitrator in a family dispute.

It is early Wednesday morning. Lucia, rubbing her eyes, comes into the classroom dragging behind her father. A teacher greets her and then comments to Lucia's father that she looks a bit tired. Sighing, he replies: "She's so difficult at home. We can't get her to eat her dinner or go to sleep at a reasonable hour. And she's always starting fights with her brother. We're exhausted. What can we do?" All at once, the teacher has gone from making an observation to being the dispenser of advice.

Each of these is a delicate situation — parents are genuinely seeking help. But they are also asking their children's teachers to go beyond what teachers can reasonably do. The requests are tempting — they complement teachers' knowledge, and often they seem like only a small extension of teachers' concern for children's development.

Backing away helpfully

Far from being trapped, teachers can take steps to help parents understand the difference between the roles of teachers, therapists, and experts — steps that clarify without abandoning or ignoring the distress or confusion that parents may feel.

1. Acknowledge what has been said. When parents open up their private lives, they make themselves vulnerable. If a teacher tries to change the topic or gloss over the issues raised, the parent may be hurt or angry. Teachers must recognize what's been revealed: "That helps me to understand why Michael has been tired. It sounds difficult for all of you."

2. Categorize the kind of problem. Once a parent has talked about a problem, a teacher must decide: Is this a classroom problem, a mild developmental issue, or an acute issue in children's or parents' lives deserving professional help?

Deciding is not always easy, but here are some examples which may help:

- **Classroom problems:** Learning to concentrate on a task; taking turns or sharing with other children; conflicts between parents and teachers over how early to start toilet training; a child's reluctance to come to school in the morning.

- **Mild family issues:** A child being unwilling to play at other children's homes; a child being afraid of monsters and refusing to go to sleep at night; parent-child conflicts over eating habits, thumb sucking, getting dressed in the morning.

- **Acute problems:** Marked delay in the child's development; extreme aggression, fears, or apathy in children; marital conflict; family abuse; severe mental or physical illness or death in the family.

It is important to categorize because teachers have the skills and information to work on classroom issues. Venturing into family issues or acute problems saddles teachers with responsibilities and demands too great to handle.

3. Make a plan for classroom issues. It is vital that parents know teachers are willing and able to work on problems of learning, behavior, and development in the classroom. Go right to work: find out what is bothering the parent, describe your view of the issue, work out joint strategies, and arrange a time to talk over progress in the near future.

4. For other kinds of problems, inform parents of other resources. If a parent brings up something other than a classroom issue, she should not be left alone with her problem neglected. Teachers can help responsibly by alerting parents to other more appropriate resources:

- **Resources for mild developmental issues:** I have seen two kinds of center-based parent resources work very well. At Eliot-Pearson, we have a parents' group led by a social worker (trained in child development), not a teacher. The group meets at the school, with no teachers or director attending. Since the group mixes parents of children of different ages and from different classrooms, the discussion doesn't turn to teachers or curriculum. Also, because of that mix, parents of younger children can learn from the mothers and fathers of older children. Parents of older children can look back and appreciate the distance they have come.

At the Brookline Early Education Project, there were specific *call-in hours* each week — just as some pediatricians have. Trained social workers and child development specialists took calls from parents concerned about issues such as sleep difficulties, sibling relationships, or changes in behavior.

■ **Resources for acute issues:** Always have a list of community resources on hand: When parents announce their needs, they are feeling them acutely. That is not the time to say: "Hmmm, I once had a friend who used a good family counselor. Let me see if I can find out what that was." Instead, it is the time to offer a well thought-out list of resources. The list should include a variety of services in a range of areas: developmental screening clinics, therapists who work with children, family therapists, marriage counselors. The list should contain services in a number of different locations and at varying levels of expense. Every resource listed must have been carefully checked.

5. Agree to collaborate. By limiting their roles, teachers aren't signing off. They can agree to work with families and outside resources to solve issues. They can work closely with parents to help children develop better eating habits or self-control. They can share information about what works in the classroom or offer observations when parents come to pick up children. They can offer to talk to a professional who will be testing the child, make it possible for that person to observe in the classroom, and meet with parents to go over any final reports.

Conclusion

The way in which teachers are pulled into acting as therapists or experts is part of a much larger situation. Families often have nowhere else to turn. Many, maybe even most, parents live apart from their own families of origin. Few pediatricians or nurses are trained to discuss and solve developmental issues. For over a century, parents have been *trained* to turn to outside experts — like Gesell or Spock — for answers. For many people, it is a large, bewildering, and expensive step to start hunting for professional help. Not surprisingly, it is teachers who inherit the flock of questions, concerns, and worries parents have.

The other side of the coin is that teachers are trained to notice and respond to the needs of other human beings. For many of them, saying "No" to a request for help feels wrong, like shutting off some very basic perception. But I am not suggesting that teachers turn a cold shoulder on families' needs. Instead, teachers should think about where they can be most helpful and where being helpful lies in pointing the way to more appropriate resources.

Penny Hauser-Cram was director of the Eliot-Pearson Children's School of Tufts University in Medford, Massachusetts, at the time this article was written.

Professionalism

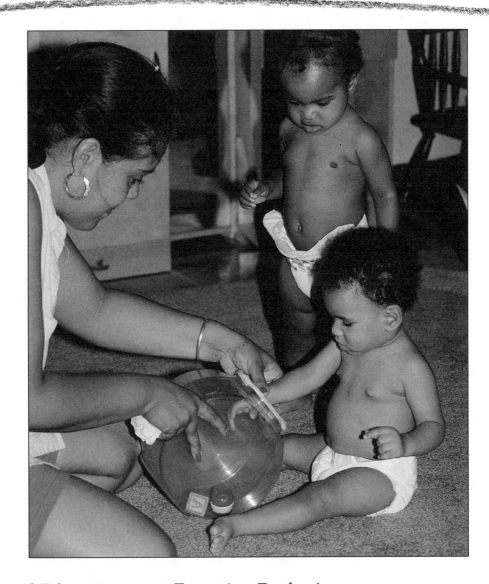

PROFESSIONALISM

Early Childhood Education as an Emerging Profession: Ongoing Conversations

by Stephanie Feeney and Nancy K. Freeman

Through our work on professional ethics in early childhood education we have had many conversations about ethics with each other, countless numbers of early childhood educators, and interested philosophers. These discussions have sometimes raised more questions than they have answered. They have, inevitably, been interesting, thought-provoking, and have helped us better understand the nature of professionalism. We will try to capture the spirit of some of these discussions as we explore what it means to be an emerging profession of women whose work involves nurturing children.

Stephanie first became involved in ethics within early childhood education in the early l980s because she knew that ethics was an important part of a profession and she wanted to help the field to become more professional. Nancy has come to the study of ethics more recently. She began by studying with Stephanie, and, since the mid-1990s, they have worked together to lead efforts to make professional ethics part of early childhood educators' repertoire.

What is a profession?

It has been almost 20 years since Stephanie began her work in ethics. That is when she met Kenneth Kipnis, a colleague at the University of Hawaii. Ken is a philosophy professor specializing in professional ethics. He and other philosophers helped early childhood educators understand the criteria used by sociologists to set professions apart from other occupations. Professions are characterized by the following attributes (Feeney, 1995; Katz, 1995; Stonehouse, 1994):

■ Requirements for entry, i.e. some selection procedure.

■ Specialized knowledge and expertise.

■ Prolonged training based on principles that involve professional judgment for their application.

■ Standards of practice that assure that every practitioner applies standard procedures in the exercise of professional judgment.

■ Distance from clients. Professionals don't "get their hands dirty" — there are intermediaries that insulate them from those they serve and who act as gatekeepers limiting clients' access to professionals in practice.

■ Commitment to a significant social value. The goal of a profession is altruistic; it is intended to meet a need in society, not to generate profit.

■ Recognition as the only group who can perform its societal function.

■ Autonomy — a profession makes its own standards, enforces itself.

■ A profession has a code of ethics. When society allows a profession to have a monopoly on a particular service they must be assured that the practitioners will behave in accordance to high moral standards. A code of ethics assures them that it will do so.

Ken also helped us appreciate the contribution an explicitly articulated code of ethics could make in our efforts to enhance the field's professionalism. He was able to describe for us, as well, a continuum of professionalism that has unskilled workers on one end and highly skilled workers on the other. With his help we began the process of figuring out where early childhood educators fit along that continuum.

Is early care and education a profession?

Our work in professional ethics has made it clear that the term *profession* is used in early care and education in two very different ways. Sometimes it is used to refer to everyone who is paid for working with young children. At other times it is reserved for those who have had a good deal of experience and education preparing them for their work.

Those who refer to all child care workers as *professionals* are highlighting the fact that caregivers working with young children deserve the prestige that is granted other professionals. We do wonder, however, if this practice doesn't do a disservice to our field, the children, and the families we serve. We believe that becoming a professional is an important goal, a distinction worth reserving for those who have devoted their time and energies to become proficient in the field. We think it worthwhile, as well, to consider how the work we do fits into the definition of professional that is recognized throughout society (Freeman, 2001). We can do that by considering how we measure up to those generally accepted criteria:

■ *We do not have rigorous requirements for entrance to training.* Admission requirements into various programs of study vary greatly and are usually determined by individual institutions. Sometimes, all that is required to enroll in specialized training is a high school diploma or GED. What's more, in many states employees who have no specialized training at all can work in educational settings with young children.

■ *We do not have professional autonomy.* Our field is regulated by laws and regulations written by legislatures and licensing boards. These bodies are made up, for the most part, of individuals who lack our specialized expertise in early care and education. Licensing is, in fact, usually regulated through states' departments of human services, and most licensing workers are trained in social work rather than early childhood education.

■ *Our professional knowledge base has become much more firmly established in recent years.* The process of codifying what we know began with the publication of *Developmentally Appropriate Practice (DAP)* in 1986. This NAEYC description of research based "best practices", while not universally acclaimed, has helped many in the field reach consensus about how to work with children from a firm base of developmental knowledge. The recent publication of two comprehensive reviews of research, *Eager to Learn* (2000) and *Neurons to Neighborhoods* (2000), has reiterated what early childhood educators have known for a long time, and has enhanced the credibility and stature of DAP in many quarters. DAP has also become the foundation for accreditation standards applied by the American Associate Degree Early Childhood Educators (ACCESS) to two-year colleges and the National Council for Accreditation of Teacher Education (NCATE) to four-year teacher education programs. As the scientific and educational communities continue to reach consensus about how children learn, early childhood

educators' specialized knowledge is gaining recognition that it has not had before.

■ *The criteria of professionalism that we most easily satisfy is altruism.* There is no doubt that we are a "career with a cause" (an informal definition of a profession). We make a contribution to society because we care for and about children. There is no doubt in anyone's mind that early childhood educators put the needs of children and families before personal gain.

■ *Because the primary recipients of our services are young and vulnerable children, it is critically important that we embrace a code of professional ethics.* The NAEYC Code of Ethical Conduct spells out our professional obligations and is widely recognized and used in our field. It makes clear our intention that high moral standards will guide our conduct. But the Code serves only as a guideline for ethical practice; there are no provisions for enforcing it. Even without enforcement mechanisms, however, it makes a valuable contribution to our credibility and our professionalism.

This consideration of the criteria that define professionals and the characteristics that describe the work of early childhood educators has led us to conclude that we are an emerging profession. It is clear that there are some criteria of professionalism, such as autonomy and selectivity, that do not apply to us. There are others we are working to achieve, such as specialized knowledge and expertise and training based on principles that involve professional judgment for their application. And some criteria, such as altruism and the existence of a code of ethics, we meet admirably. We believe that not only are we an emerging profession, but we are also an evolving one. We are unique, in part, because we are a profession of women, shaped by women's values and ways of interacting with each other, the children, and the families with whom we work.

What does it mean to be a profession of nurturing women?

In the ethics workshops we have conducted since the 1980s and in our articles and books devoted to ethics we've asked early childhood educators to analyze commonly-occurring, real life dilemmas faced by early childhood educators. We have used cases like the one describing Timothy's mother's request that his teacher not let him nap in school (Katz, 1987; Feeney & Freeman, 1999).

In one of the first workshops Ken facilitated with Stephanie, he commented that the participants (all women) reacted completely differently to ethical dilemmas than did the mostly male professionals with whom he usually worked. He noted that early childhood educators did not come to quick conclusions the way doctors and lawyers did. Instead, they wanted to discuss every situation and to explore every possible variable at length.

What's more, they asked for a great deal of background information and put off making any decision as long as they could. For example, when they considered the dilemma created by Tim's mother's request, they wanted to know what the child had eaten for breakfast, if the teacher tried letting him play at naptime, what we knew about the family's bedtime routines. And even when they had lots of information, early childhood educators were reluctant to make ethical decisions and wouldn't do so unless pressed by workshop leaders. When urged to make a definitive judgment in a case, the participants would invariably explain that they didn't want to discount any viewpoint or make anyone feel like they had been the loser. They always tried to find a way for everyone to win and to feel good about the situation.

These observations led us to revisit the writings of Carol Gilligan (1993), Nel Noddings (1984, 1990) and others who have studied how women work through life's difficult decisions. We found it helpful to be reminded, once again, of what Gilligan refers to as women's "different voice" — their particular ways of understanding the world, their place in it, and their relationships with colleagues, family, and friends at home and in the workplace. Gilligan asserts that women define themselves through these relationships and their connections to other people more than do men, who tend to focus on protecting individuals' rights, on what is fair and equitable.

It is this sensitivity to the needs of others and the tendency to assume the responsibility for taking care of others, that leads women to include in their day-to-day personal and professional decisions the voices, the perspectives, of others. Women tend to see the relationship rather than the individual as primary. Gilligan uses the term the "ethic of care" to describe this characteristically feminine approach to moral judgment and the "ethic of justice" to describe the more typically masculine approach. While Gilligan's work has been criticized for lacking empirical proof of its validity, it has certainly provided great insight into what we have observed in the ethics workshops we have conducted over the years.

Noddings' work, likewise, contributes to our understanding of women's approaches to professional ethics. She describes the ethic of care which "emphasizes needs over rights and love over duty" (Noddings, 1990). Noddings helps us understand that caring is something we do, not something we are. It is not simply warm hugs and gentle smiles but involves, instead, the hard work of giving our full attention to another and putting their needs before our own (Goldstein, 1998). Caring puts human connections at the heart of all relationships and responsibilities. Noddings reminds us, as well, that caring is not just for women, but guides all who believe compassion, caring, and connection will make the world a better place.

In our experience, women in early childhood education respond to ethical dilemmas with primary concern for the people and relationships involved, rather than with emphasis on fairness which is more typical of male professionals. If we approach moral dilemmas in different ways than male professionals, then it stands to reason that women in a female dominated profession will approach becoming a profession differently than those in male dominated professions.

At this time in our history, we appear to be somewhere in the middle of the continuum of professionalism. We aspire to some of the characteristics of other professions. Why wouldn't we want the pay, power, and prestige that comes with professional status? Early childhood educators today recognize the benefits of helping those outside our field to recognize our specialized knowledge, and wish to add our voices to conversations involving program regulations and certification requirements (Freeman, 2001). And, of course, we enthusiastically support efforts to provide those who work in early care and education worthy wages and fair benefits. But the cost of a profession might well be too great for us to embrace all the characteristics listed above. Most early childhood educators wouldn't consider creating a professional distance or "keeping our hands clean" philosophy for example; that would be compromising what we know about working effectively with young children and their families.

Where do we go from here?

We are caught on the horns of a very real dilemma. On one hand we would like to have the recognition, respect, and compensation that comes with professional status. On the other hand we are committed to maintaining the caring, inclusive, democratic, and humanistic traditions that make us proud to be early childhood educators. At this time in our history we need to keep asking ourselves how a field guided by the values and styles of interaction that characterize nurturing women can successfully negotiate the terrain of professionalism. We reconcile this conflict by envisioning a different kind of profession, one that occupies a unique position along the continuum of professionalism that lets us preserve the values that we cherish while gaining the recognition (and compensation) that our very significant contributions to society deserve. We wish for a field where early childhood educators' expertise is recognized, where all earn worthy wages, and where the prestige of being a professional is conferred on all who posses the necessary knowledge and expertise. We believe it is our challenge to create a profession that is like a grandmother's patchwork quilt — one that is carefully crafted to reflect our history and traditions; warm and nurturing, big enough for colleagues who bring varied experience and education, and so well designed that it is admired by both those within and outside of our professional family.

We hope you will join the conversation at the local, state, and national levels, helping both those within and beyond our field appreciate the expertise, experience, and commitment of those who care for our youngest and most vulnerable citizens. We wish that parents, the public, policy makers, and politicians would consider early childhood education to be a unique kind of profession and hope you will join efforts to make that wish a reality.

References

Bromer, J. (2001). Helpers, mothers, and preachers: The multiple roles and discourses of family child care providers in an African-American community. *Early Childhood Research Quarterly, 16,* 313-327.

Feeney, S. (1995). Professionalism in early childhood teacher education: Focus on ethics. *Journal of Early Childhood Teacher Education, 16*(3):13-15.

Feeney, S., & Freeman, N. K. (1999). *Ethics and the early childhood educator: Using the NAEYC Code.* Washington, DC: National Association for the Education of Young Children.

Feeney, S., & Kipnis, K. (1989/1998). *Code of ethical conduct and statement of commitment.* Washington, DC: National Association for the Education of Young Children.

Freeman, N. K. (2001). Early childhood education: Tools for becoming a profession. *Dimensions of Early Childhood, 29*(3), 11-17.

Gilligan, C. (1993). In a different voice: *Psychological theory and women's development.* Revised ed. Cambridge, MA: Harvard University Press.

Goldstein, L. S. (1998). More than gentle smiles and warm hugs: Applying the ethic of care to early childhood education. *Journal of Research in Childhood Education, 12*(2), 244-261.

Katz, L. G. (1987). Ethics Commission member's comment. In Ethics case studies: The working mother. *Young Children, 43*(1):18.

Katz, L. G. (1995). *Talks with teachers of young children.* Norwood, NJ: Ablex.

National Research Council (2000). *Eager to learn: Educating our preschoolers.* Committee on Early Childhood Pedagogy. Barbara Bowman, M. Suzanne Donovan, & M. Susan Burns, eds. Commission on Behavioral and Social Sciences and Education. Washington, DC: National Academy Press

National Research Council and Institute of Medicine (2000). *From neurons to neighborhoods: The science of early childhood development.* Committee on Integrating the Science of Early Childhood Development. Jack P. Shonkoff and Deborah A. Phillips, eds. Board on Children, Youth and Families, Commission on Behavioral and Social Sciences Education. Washington, DC: National Academy Press.

Noddings, N. (1984). *Caring: A feminine approach to ethics and morality.* Berkeley, CA: University of California Press.

Noddings, N. (1990). Ethics from the standpoint of women. *Theoretical perspectives on sexual differences.* Edited by Deborah L. Rhode. New Haven, CT: Yale University Press.

Stonehouse, A. (1994). *Not just nice ladies.* Castle Hill, New South Wales, Australia: Pademelon Press.

Stephanie Feeney is Professor of Education Emerita at the University of Hawaii at Manoa. She is co-author of the *NAEYC Code of Ethical Conduct* and two books on professional ethics: *Ethics and the Early Childhood Educator: Using the NAEYC Code of Ethics,* (with Nancy Freeman), and *Teaching the NAEYC Code of Ethical Conduct* (with Nancy Freeman and Eva Moravcik). Her other publications include the textbook *Who Am I in the Lives of Children?,* a curriculum for young children, four children's books about Hawaii, and numerous articles.

Nancy K. Freeman, Ph.D. is an associate professor of early childhood education and research director of the Children's Center at the University of South Carolina. She has been a preschool teacher, a child care program director, and has written two books (with Stephanie Feeney), and several articles about the ethics of early childhood education.

Using Beginnings Workshop to Train Teachers by Kay Albrecht

Worth considering: Do teachers in your school consider themselves professionals? Work with the list of characteristics of professions with teachers, considering their ideas and responses to each characteristic. Do your teachers reach the same conclusion as Feeney and Freeman, or not? Reflecting about issues like this may be a new experience for teachers. Practice thinking about big issues like this one is a milestone in becoming a practicing professional and worth the effort it may take to do so.

Enlightening practice: For teachers who have not been exposed to ethical thinking, use one of the case studies published in *Young Children* or in Feeney's books (see reference list) to explore an ethical issue at a staff meeting. After this first exposure, take an issue that is affecting someone on your faculty and explore it from an ethical perspective (Chapter 3, Addressing Ethical Issues, in *Ethics and the Early Childhood Educator* will give you guidance in doing this). This type of experience is reflective practice at its best!

PROFESSIONALISM

Voices in Search of Cultural Continuity in Communities

A dialogue between Marion Hironaka Cowee, Kim Statum Francisco, Moraima Mendoza, and Carol Mills facilitated by Cecelia Alvarado

As we consider the concept of professionalism, it is important to realize that different ethnic/cultural communities may have different ways of relating to the concept and different expectations of the professionals with whom they work and who care for their children. With this in mind, I was privileged to interview four early care and education professionals, who come from communities of color, in a variety of locations across the country. I have known and worked with each of them in different professional contexts, over a number of years, and have found them to be among the most earnest, critical thinkers I know.

My questions to them focused on three main areas of inquiry: 1) the differences between the mainstream, European-American concept of professionalism and that of their own community; 2) the characteristics — behaviors, attitudes, values — that people of color look for in the professionals who are serving their families; and 3) the implications for training professionals of color or those who will work in communities of color.

In hopes that the richness of their responses will stimulate the reader to consider different paradigms, cultural contexts, and ways of delivering services to children and parents, I offer the following excerpts from our conversation with one caution — that is, that each of these women is speaking from her own experience and cultural context. They do not intend to speak for all members of their ethnic/cultural groups, and each acknowledges great variation among the populations from which they come. However, the similarities we will find between these perspectives of women of color and those specific to each group, should give each of us pause to consider these points when working with the communities represented in this dialogue.

The concept of professionalism in communities of color

The concept of professionalism appears to be a mainstream construct, one that comes from outside the experiences of the Latino, Japanese, African-American, and Wampanoag communities of these four women. Their responses to the term differ slightly but reveal common themes.

The Latinos that Moraima works with don't feel comfortable with the use of the word *professional*, as it infers "acting superior." Kim reports that her community "clearly has individuals that are successful in professional life (traditional paths re: degrees, etc.), but legitimate status also comes from their local small business development and church-based leadership roles that may not entail owning wealth and degrees."

In the Native community where Carol lives, the term *professional* has negative connotations. Members of her community often perceive a professional as not having "cultural, traditional, family ways." She notes that her community "does not always readily trust in existing mainstream institutions and, therefore, may have a lack of understanding of systems and services. The *white tape* bureaucracy sometimes produces professionals that may act in a demanding, humiliating manner that leaves community members feeling degraded and confused."

Marion perceives that her community of Japanese-Americans views professionals from within their community as, " . . . more down to earth, less having to live up to image, emotionally connected (one's behavior is affected by people and lives of those present), organic/not packaged." She senses a conflict between the philosophy to "Don't overstate your reach by saying you can take on things that you haven't done before," as her Sansei (third) generation has been taught by the Nisei (second generation), and the larger European-American mainstream expectation that one is supposed to "sell themselves" in their profession.

Clearly, within European-American communities there may also be some of these sentiments, but the point here is that the generally accepted, positive notion of *professional* as used in our field is seen quite differently in these communities.

Characteristics that people of color look for in the professionals who serve their families

Carol observes that "trust and confidentiality" are the most important characteristics for professionals to bring to "small communities that have a fear of not being able to have either." Says Carol, "Being loving, not as structured, not rigid in discipline, casual, flexible in time allowances and emergency and family matters" are essential characteristics if a professional is to be effective and accepted in the Wampanoag community. Keeping talking to a minimum is also viewed positively. Often, Carol's community perceives professionals from other communities as bringing a strong emphasis on verbal communication: "So much talking." In contrast, the Native way values "a respect for silence and other ways of communicating, utilizing body movement to show approval or disapproval." Carol notes that early childhood teachers from outside the community seem to use words such as "Good job!" even when "a child's action itself is rewarding."

Kim believes that, "children need to be where they are respected and adored." In the African-American communities of Kim's experience, a respected professional in the early childhood field is evaluated by her interaction with children and families, "Do I see folk comfortable as people of color and do they translate that to children? What mode of discipline do they use? Can I see my child here?" Kim continues, "Building a strong personal relationship with each parent, interacting genuinely, encouraging parental involvement, and accepting them, fully, with whatever life situations they bring is also critically important to building trust."

Marion reflects that, "being approachable, respectful, listening to others, not intimidating, kind, down home, and cooperative rather than competitive" are important traits of professionals who work in the Japanese community. She continues that sometimes professionals from outside the community present "certain behaviors and a visual perception (smooth) that results in an emotional disconnect" for families.

Moraima advises that successful professionals in the Latino community are recognized because, "they bring lots of knowledge and skills and they are accessible. They have the attitude that we are all teachers and learners. They involve people, and they don't keep a distance. Whites sometimes give the message, 'Don't get too close, I'm just here to get the information.' Meetings are often rigid — not set-up for participation. Time is an issue; hold your comments to the end."

Implications for training of professionals from communities of color or others who will work in them

"My experience in mainstream society is that theory and philosophy are often treated as more important than relationships,"
offers Marion. "It is true that we should be proud to have a well-articulated philosophy in our programs, but I find that when teachers of color bring something different, it may not be valued. There is no dialogue about this. Teachers are emotionally discounted if they have different cultural values. I have worked in mainstream centers that expected me to give up the nurturing part of myself (not to do anything for children that they could do for themselves) because they valued independence. I value interdependence — and I felt uncomfortable being who I am and relating in ways that felt culturally inconsistent to who I am. At the time, I was not clear about the exact issues. I knew it didn't feel right, but I couldn't identify the issues of power and I couldn't talk about the cultural conflict. I'm sure that the directors and others never intended for me to feel stifled and powerless, but I did feel that way. They had strong, principled programs and I have no doubt that they wanted to meet the needs of the children, but my need to respond from my culturally authentic place was neither encouraged nor valued."

So, what are the implications/suggested strategies for training professionals for our field? Suggested strategies from Kim for developing professionals for her community include the following:

■ In your recruitment efforts, contact people personally (as opposed to using flyers) about training being offered.

■ Ask community professionals what they need in terms of professional development (don't assume you know).

■ Be flexible in accommodating the needs of individuals and their families.

Marion adds:

■ Respect the subtleties of cultural practices (such as in Japanese communities, avoiding confrontational situations, taking someone aside as opposed to raising an issue in a staff meeting).

■ Allow people with different perspectives to voice them without being labeled *troublemaker* (e.g., "When you are not so angry, come back.").

Carol offers:

■ Avoid the attitude of superiority that is present when we value book knowledge over knowledge of our elders (the wisdom of nature, time, and experience).

■ Support natural time schedules (seasons, our body systems, etc.) as opposed to always promoting *clock* time.

■ Allow for slower processing/thinking before talking, that some groups may need.

Moraima contributes:

- If we want people to receive the full benefits of the professional development we provide, it should be offered in the language in which they think and they understand.

- With Latinos and some other people of color, realize that the term *professional* brings with it a lot of baggage. It may be preferable to speak about building a person's competence to provide culturally appropriate services and effectively advocate for families.

In search of cultural continuity in communities, spend additional time at the beginning of a meeting to inquire about the health of family members before moving to the agenda. Invite respected elders in a community to offer timeless wisdom about child rearing practices. Offer training in a language other than English — practices not usually a part of the professional development of providers. Most importantly, take the time to listen, ask questions, and try new ways of being.

Cecelia Alvarado is a senior associate at the Wheelock College Institute for Leadership and Career Initiatives in Boston, Massachusetts. Former chairperson of the Early Childhood Education Department at Santa Barbara City College and Past President of California AEYC, her current work is focused on leadership development, faculty development, and diversifying the leadership of the field.

Marion Hironaka Cowee is Japanese-American, works as a member of the early childhood education faculty at Solano Community College in Fairfield, California.

Moraima Mendoza is a Latina working at the Spanish American Union, Springfield, Massachusetts, as the early care and education director and director of the Latino Family Child Care Association.

Carol Mills is Ojibway, living in a community of largely Wampanoag Native people in Mashpee, Massachusetts, who works for Cape Cod Child Development, Early Intervention, as an education specialist and is also a training and technical assistance consultant for Head Start and Early Head Start.

Kim Statum Francisco is African-American, and is the project director of Parents as Partners in Education, Oklahoma City, Oklahoma.

Using Beginnings Workshop to Train Teachers by Kay Albrecht

Cultural Continuity in Your Center: Replicate the rich exchange of information shared here in your school. Identify staff members or parents who represent diverse cultures who are willing to help add cultural insight into the three main areas of inquiry addressed in the article (see p. 29). Share the article with teachers and schedule an uninterrupted time for your panel to respond to the three areas of inquiry. Follow this replication with a discussion among teachers identifying areas of similarities and differences and how insights might be added or included in interactions, curricula, or policies and procedures.

Including Cultural Differences in Philosophies: Cowee brings up an interesting dilemma related to philosophy statements (see p. 30). Are there avenues to discuss cultural conflicts that are created by cultural variations among staff and parents? Do you give teachers a chance to reflect on your school's philosophy statement and identify cultural variations that might need to be included or modified? Analyzing your school's philosophy statement in light of cultural differences or variations would be a great follow-up activity to the replication activity above.

Cultural Continuity Survey: Consider conducting a survey of the characteristics that your families consider important in professionals like the one suggested by Alvarado (see p. 30). Use the results to help teachers understand how they are viewed differently by parents representing different cultural groups. Follow this with a candid discussion with teachers about how they might modify their professional behaviors to reflect these variations.

PROFESSIONALISM

Early Childhood Professionals: Current Status and Projected Needs

by Ann Epstein

Because qualified early childhood staff are so critical to children's development, the national concern about the shortage of professional personnel is well founded. In order to make responsible decisions, policymakers require accurate data about the population and preparation of the nation's teachers and child care providers. This article summarizes what we know about the field's current status and projected needs, including numbers in the workforce, education and training, compensation, and turnover. It presents this data in the context of our research knowledge about what is best for young children, their families, and those who serve them.

Current status

It is widely accepted that well-trained and well-compensated staff are key determinants of early childhood program quality and healthy child development. *Eager to Learn*, a publication of the National Academy of Sciences (2000), summarizes evidence that "social competence and school achievement are influenced by the quality of early teacher-child relationships, and by teachers' attentiveness to how the child approaches learning" (p. 6). Positive teacher and caregiver qualities are in turn most strongly correlated with their years of formal schooling and their specialized training in early childhood education and development. How close are we to meeting the ideal of a sizable early childhood workforce prepared to support children's development?

Current number of teachers and providers. In response to the demand for child care, the number of providers has increased threefold in the last two decades. The U.S. Bureau of Labor Statistics (2001) reports that in 1999 (the latest year for which complete data is available and analyzed) there were 662,882 employees in the category of "child day care services." Preliminary 2001 data indicate the number of child care employees has increased an additional 16% in the last two years, to a total of 770,000 providers. This figure does not include Head

Start, which counts an additional 94,000 teachers and 5,000 home visitors (Head Start Bureau, 2001). Officials at the National Center for the Early Childhood Workforce speculate that the number of child care workers in the U.S. today may realistically approach two million by the time unregulated family child care providers are taken into account (National Conference of State Legislatures, 1995).

Current education and training status. Levels of education among early childhood staff have increased in the last two decades, attributable in part to professionalization campaigns by the National Association for the Education of Young Children (NAEYC) and Head Start. The number of center-based teachers with four-year college degrees has grown from 29 percent to nearly 50 percent (Willer, Hofferth, Kisker, Divine-Hawkins, Farquhar, & Glantz, 1991). Recent data from the Head Start Family and Child Experiences Survey (FACES) indicated that 49 percent of Head Start teachers had undergraduate degrees and 15 percent had graduate degrees (U.S. Department of Health and Human Services, 1999).

In addition to higher levels of general education, more teachers and providers are receiving training specific to the field. The National Household Education Survey reported that 58 percent of the children in out-of-home care had primary providers with child development training (Hofferth, Shauman, Henke, & West, 1998). Training varied according to the type of setting: providers in center-based programs (95%) were most likely to have relevant training, followed by family child care providers (48%), in-home child care providers (33%), and relative care (18%). While public school teachers are more like to have formal degrees, Head Start teachers are more likely to have early childhood training (Epstein, 1993). The Head Start Bureau (2001) reports that 93 percent of its teachers have degrees in early childhood education or are obtaining training for the Child Development Associate (CDA) credential or state preschool certification. To the extent that Head Start serves as a national laboratory for the early childhood field as a whole, levels of education and training among staff in general can be expected to increase in the coming decade.

Another encouraging finding is that parents appear to increasingly value caregiver training in choosing child care settings. Three-quarters of the over 14,000 parents interviewed in the National Household Education Survey said having a provider trained in child care was important in their choice, outranking small class size, reasonable cost, proximity to home, and provision of care for sick children. "In addition, training is the one quality characteristic for which parents apparently pay more and [that] is linked with parents' choice of arrangement. Since training is viewed by the child development community as a key component of quality child care, these findings offer promising signals that parental preferences and child development experts' recommendations diverge less than believed" (Hofferth et al., 1998, p. 10).

Current compensation levels. Child care providers "earn less than half as much as comparably educated women and less than one-third as much as comparably educated men" (Whitebook, Phillips, & Howes, 1993, p. 10). The average salary of child care workers is only $15,430 a year, less than the yearly salaries for funeral attendants, bellhops, and garbage collectors (Children's Defense Fund, 2001). Yet there is a challenge in trying to upgrade their professional status: licensing regulations often hold minimal educational requirements so wages are low. With low wages, the field cannot attract or retain qualified personnel. Although real wages for the highest paid teachers have risen slightly in the last decade, those for teaching assistants, the fastest growing segment of the child care workforce, have actually declined (National Conference of State Legislators, 1995). The benefit picture is equally discouraging; only 30 percent of child care teachers receive job benefits such as health insurance or paid vacations and sick leave.

Current turnover rates. Staff turnover is a major problem in early care and education programs. According to the Center for the Child Care Workforce, annual turnover rates are 30 percent even in the best of programs, 40 percent in the field as a whole, and 50 percent among center directors (Whitebook et al., 1989 & 2001). When staff members leave, only half continue to work in child care, and their replacements often have significantly lower education levels. Not surprisingly, higher wages help reduce turnover rates. Other organizational factors, particularly a commitment to staff development, can also help improve tenure rates (Bloom, 1988). Head Start, the auspice with the greatest support for inservice training, has the lowest turnover rates, followed by public schools, non profit settings, and for profit agencies, respectively (Epstein, 1993).

Projected needs

Although research offers substantial evidence about what works for programs and children, there is often a missing link between knowledge and practice — sometimes called "the professional development gap." To close this gap, the field needs training methods and public policies that attract and retain a pool of talented and committed staff. Concerns about future needs, therefore, revolve around quantity and, above all, quality.

Number of teachers and providers needed. In estimating the number of caregivers needed, a critical variable is the number of children each adult can effectively supervise and support. The NAEYC 1998 accreditation standards recommend ratios of 1:8 to 1:10 for preschoolers and 1:3 to 1:5 for infants and toddlers. According to the National Center for Education Statistics, there are an estimated 13 million young children in out-of-home care, including 8 million preschoolers and 5 million infants and toddlers (U.S. Department of Education, 2000). Based on these figures, the nation needs 800,000 to 1 million caregivers for preschoolers and 1 to 1.67 million caregivers for infants and toddlers. The 662,882 child care workers recorded by the U.S. Department of Labor Statistics (2001) obviously falls far short of the needed number, suggesting that: a) the field has many undocumented workers, and b) the actual number of children per caregiver far exceeds the recommended adult-child ratios.

Need for teacher-training programs. Exacerbating the problem of an inadequate number of teachers and caregivers is a shortage of training facilities. A survey by the National Center for Early Learning and Development concluded that today's 1,200 teacher-training programs will not have an adequate number of faculty to meet projected workforce needs (Early & Winton, 2001). Preservice teacher-preparation programs will need a 76 percent increase in early childhood faculty if a bachelor's degree becomes a prerequisite for employment in the field.

Inservice training for current personnel is an alternative pathway for improving program quality. Several studies demonstrate that this option is particularly valuable for those who enter the field with the lowest levels of formal education, such as Head Start teachers and child care providers (Epstein, 1999; Layzer, et al., 1993). Some types of inservice training can be delivered through collaborative arrangements with institutions of higher learning. However, the most effective staff development models employ personnel from within the early childhood agency who can provide continuity and onsite observation and feedback to teachers and caregivers (National Academy of Sciences, 2000).

People such as program directors, education and curriculum specialists, and teacher supervisors are in the best position to provide training to staff members in their agencies (Epstein,

1993). Unfortunately, the financial resources available for agency-based training are generally limited to certain settings and populations, such as public school prekindergarten or Head Start programs (Adams & Poersch, 1997). Those agencies that could most benefit from this type of inservice training, such as for-profit child care centers, are often the ones least able to pay for on-staff trainers or cover the time and substitute costs for caregivers to attend the training.

Need for training in child development and early childhood pedagogy. Research offers clear guidelines on the content of staff development initiatives. Training should be comprehensive and integrate theory with practice, addressing both the *why* and *how* of program implementation. The first essential component of teacher preparation is a thorough grounding in all dimensions of early childhood development, including physical growth, emotional and affective development, social development, language and literacy development, cognition, and creativity. The second part of training must translate this child development knowledge into appropriate classroom practices. Teachers and caregivers need specific research-based strategies to implement high quality programs that incorporate the following elements:

- supportive adult-child interactions;
- safe and stimulating learning environments;
- consistent yet flexible daily routines;
- diverse experiences that address a range of social and academic content areas;
- sensitivity to individual differences;
- sensitivity to group differences;
- creating a bridge between the program and children's families and communities;
- effective team work; and
- child and program assessment.

Need for effective training strategies. In addition to considering the *training content* (child development and pedagogy), staff preparation must also consider the *training process*. Highly effective training programs "actively engage teachers and provide high-quality supervision. Teachers are encouraged to reflect on their practice and on the responsive-ness of their children to classroom activities, and to revise and plan their teaching accordingly" (National Academy of Sciences, 2000, p. 7). Decades of research on adult learning tell us that effective teacher-training models include the following:

- active involvement by participants;
- integration of theory and practice;
- distributive learning instead of disconnected workshops;
- a consistent trainer who works with staff over time;
- follow-up classroom visits; and
- sharing and reflection among staff.

Need for improved compensation and working conditions. Since education and job-related training are the primary justification for higher compensation, the starting point in launching an upward cycle is to encourage and preferably mandate these background requirements. *Eager to Learn* offers two relevant recommendations — a teacher with a bachelor's degree for each group of children and a single career ladder for early childhood professionals that progresses from assistants with CDAs to teachers with bachelor's degrees to supervisors with graduate training (National Academy of Sciences, 2000). Meeting these dual needs for better teacher education and career paths will require a substantial public awareness campaign and commitment to public investment. Without this expenditure, however, we cannot hope to reach and reward optimal levels of professional development in the early childhood arena.

References

Adams, G. C., & Poersch, N. O. (1997). *Key facts about child care and early education: A briefing book*. Washington, DC: Children's Defense Fund.

Bloom, P. J. (1988). Factors influencing overall job commitment and satisfaction in early childhood work environments. *Journal of Research in Childhood Education, 3*(2), 107-122.

Children's Defense Fund. (2001). *The state of America's children: 2001 yearbook*. Washington, DC: Author.

Early, D., & Winton, P. (2001, in press). Preparing the workforce: Early childhood teacher preparation at 2- and 4-year institutions of higher learning. *Early Childhood Research Quarterly*.

Epstein, A. S. (1993). *Training for quality: Improving early childhood programs through systematic inservice training*. Ypsilanti, MI: High/Scope Press.

Epstein, A. S. (1999). Pathways to quality in Head Start, public school, and private non-profit early childhood programs. *Journal of Research in Childhood Education, 13*(2), 101-119.

Head Start Bureau. (2001). *Head Start 2000 Statistical Fact Sheet*. Washington, DC: U.S. Department of Health and Human Services.

Hofferth, S. L., Shauman, K. A., Henke, R. R., & West, J. (June, 1998). *Characteristics of children's early care and education programs: Data from the 1995 National Household Education Survey*. Washington, DC: U.S. Department of Education, National Center for Education Statistics.

Layzer, J. I., Goodson, B. D., & Moss, M. (1993). *Observational Study of Early Childhood Programs, Final Report Volume 1: Life in Preschool*. Washington, DC: U.S. Department of Education.

National Academy of Sciences. (2000). *Eager to learn: Educating our preschoolers.* Washington, DC: National Academy Press.

National Association for the Education of Young Children. (1998). *Accreditation criteria and procedures.* Washington, DC: Author.

National Conference of State Legislatures. (1995). *Early childhood care and education: An investment that works.* Washington, DC: Author.

U.S. Bureau of Labor Statistics. (2001). *Survey output.* Washington, DC: Author. Available on the Web at http://stats.bls.gov/datahome.htm.

U.S. Department of Education, National Center for Education Statistics. (2000). *Digest of education statistics.* Washington, DC: Author.

U.S. Department of Health & Human Services. (January, 1999). *Family and Child Experiences Survey (FACES) Second-Year Report.*

Presented at Consortium of Head Start Quality Research Centers, Washington, D.C.

Whitebook, M., Howes, C., & Phillips, D. (1989). *Who cares? Child care teachers and the quality of care in America.* Oakland, CA: Child Care Employee Project.

Whitebook, M., Phillips, D., & Howes, C. (1993). *National child care staffing study revisited: Four years in the life of center-based child care.* Oakland, CA: Child Care Employee Project.

Whitebook, M., Sakai, L., Gerber, E., & Howes, C. (2001). *Then and now: Changes in child care staffing, 1994-2000.* Washington, DC: Center for the Child Care Workforce.

Willer, B., Hofferth, S. L., Kisker, E. E., Divine-Hawkins, P., Farquhar, E., & Glantz, F. (1991). *The demand and supply of child care in 1990.* Washington, DC: National Association for the Education of Young Children.

Ann S. Epstein is the director of the early childhood division at the High/Scope Educational Research Foundation where she has worked on curriculum development, staff training, and research and evaluation projects since 1975. She has a Ph.D. in Developmental Psychology from the University of Michigan and is the author of numerous books and articles on early childhood development, staff training, and program evaluation.

Using Beginnings Workshop to Train Teachers by Kay Albrecht

Mean, Median, or Mode?: Epstein shares a large number of characteristics of the early childhood professional workforce. Compare your center to some of the categories she covers to see where your school falls in the larger picture of our profession. Categories that might prove useful include current level of education and training (see p. 32); current compensation rates (see p. 33); and current turnover rates (see p. 33). Use these comparisons to make an action plan.

Validation and Challenge!: Epstein validates that program directors, education and curriculum specialists, and teacher supervisors are in the best position to provide appropriate and timely training to teachers — something many of us already knew intuitively. She also recognizes that financial resources for providing effective training are usually scarce. Explore ways this valuable training might be provided with limited resources and get teachers to help identify priorities for where to start.

For Directors Only: Epstein's calculation of the number of new faculty needed is staggering (see p. 33). Where will you find your share of these new workers? Make a long term, continuous recruitment plan to insure that your school will be staffed adequately with well credentialed and trained teachers. Implement your plan now!!

How Do I Relate and Share Professionally?

by Rhonda Forrest and Nadine McCrea

Our values and beliefs underpin the way we act and respond to others. Therefore, a reflective journey that deepens our self-awareness is essential to improving ways we communicate and provide foundations for establishing and maintaining relationships. Professionals need to take responsibility for sharing understandings with the field and wider society. By entering into professional debates about early childhood education, we can influence political, professional, and scholarly spheres.

Relating with others

Deepening values and beliefs. Our professional identities are in part founded on our evolving values and beliefs. This means that our past philosophical notions of early childhood education continue to shape our contemporary ideals and actions. We base our actions in values that may or may not be explicit or clearly understood. Therefore, as part of understanding our own professional foundations, it is essential that we uncover and consider the deep-seated notions that steer and motivate us. This exploration of self can expose personally held concepts that often surprise and may shock us.

Sometimes we hold beliefs which, when tested in real life situations, are inadequate for effective decision making and, therefore, are revealed as simplistic. Often these situations highlight ethical dilemmas, which involve opposing but defensible alternatives (Feeney & Freeman, 1999). For example, you might place the legitimate interests of a child above the rights of the parent or you may decide to protect the rights of a group of children even when this means that the options for one child become restricted. Here, as a professional, you are required to balance the interests and rights of one against the other. Encountering such dilemmas means that all of us must move beyond shallowly held beliefs and actually think deeply about the people who are involved.

Along this challenging journey, professionals can make use of a number of supportive documents and processes. Two significant documents are Codes of Ethics (AECA, 1990; Feeney & Freeman, 1999) and the United Nations Declaration of the Rights of the Child (Waters, 1998). Processes that can assist us include developing personal philosophies (Morrison, 1997), dealing with ethical dilemmas (Feeney & Freeman, 1999), and being reflective professionals.

Reflecting purposefully. Reflective practitioners critically appraise their professional understandings. There are different forms of reflection including technical rationality, practical action, and critical reflection (van Manen, 1977; cited in Zeichner & Liston, 1987). These concepts are pivotal to moving from a basic level of reading for meaning, thinking, and writing through to complex, more advanced metacognitive processes that are expected of professionals. Technical rationality involves the unquestioning use of knowledge to attain defined ends. The next level, practical action, involves analysing assumptions about daily actions and deciding to act based on their practicality. We encourage you to move to critical reflection which is based on asking moral and ethical questions that lead to just and equitable social outcomes.

A reflective journal can document your professional journey. It is a place where you record your thinking about complex issues. Journal writing represents communicating with yourself about who you are and what you do in your educational setting. This can happen at any or all of van Manen's reflective levels. Writing may generate ideas and emotions about changing yourself and the organisation you work in. It is a mode of active learning for deeper understanding. Revisiting earlier entries to see how your thinking has changed may be a useful check of your values and beliefs. In structuring your journal you might like to incorporate (Fulwiler, 1987):

Activities for exploring team relationships:

1. Write a 300 word personal introduction of yourself under the following headings:
   - Who am I?
   - Where have I come from?
   - How and why does understanding myself effect the way I relate to others?

2. Begin in groups of three to five and brainstorm your values and beliefs about relating and interacting with colleagues. Secondly, record your collective thoughts in a mind map and discuss these. Then, individually identify how your values have just influenced the way you related with the group in this activity. Record your reflective responses for transcribing into your journal.

3. Imagine that you are newly arrived in your current workplace. You need to communicate effectively with parents and staff. Identify and profile your stakeholders: Who are they? What do they need to know about you that will help you work more effectively? Then, design an oral presentation to introduce yourself to this audience. Share your draft presentation with another team member.

4. In pairs, reflect on the team development needs of your organization. Formulate an action plan that assists you to: identify and prioritise these needs; arrange regular time for team development; and, justify to your employer why she should allocate funds for these activities.

- informal, even colloquial diction;
- the first person pronoun 'I';
- informal punctuation;
- informal rhythms of every day speech; and
- informal experimentation.

Establishing and maintaining relationships. Because early childhood education is people focused, how we relate to adults and children is pivotal to our professionalism. Our way of relating emanates from many forms of communication, which may be verbal, non-verbal, or written. Hence, communication involves aspects of power and position and attitudes about our relationships with others. We can understand and improve our relationships by reflecting on how we communicate and refine such skills as effective listening.

Communication and relationships in the early childhood field are complex as they involve a variety of people with different levels of power and influence. Consider whether you relate to staff, parents, and children in encouraging, supportive, collaborative, or cooperative ways regardless of their status. Staff relationships are often volatile, so relating within a team may be particularly challenging. As a professional educator, reflect on your effectiveness as a team member. Ask yourself: Am I encouraging? Am I supportive and understanding of the perspectives of others? How do I relate during difficult moments? Do my comments alienate some staff or do they help resolve conflicts?

Sharing with others

Engaging in professional debate. We have already highlighted that the journey of relating professionally begins with self-awareness. Next, we consider how we share our work lives in professional ways. We can do this by actively engaging in webs of influence, which are the political web, professional web, and the scholarly web (Meade, 1995 cited in Rodd, 1997). This means that individually or collectively we share by: advocating for policies within the political web; debating professionalization within the professional web; and guiding practice through the scholarly web.

In order to share our professionalism we must recognise that our beliefs are evolving and our global context is "discontinuously changing" (Limerick & Cunnington, 1993). This means that change is not predictable but tends to come out of left field. If we embrace change, we can collectively influence the directions of our profession rather than being constrained by outdated traditions (Morrison, 1994). We must recognise that within our people-centered profession we need people with heart who can navigate the currents of change so that the profession is steered toward wise practice (McCrea, 2000). In order for each of us to be such a professional, we need to examine our hearts, develop heart-driven advocacy skills, and share our understandings.

Sharing through advocating. Having the heart to improve the early childhood profession is a solid foundation for becoming an advocate. Knowledge and expertise can be learned and needs to be shared, if we are to participate in shaping our profession. This path can begin with a belief in our *possible selves* and a commitment of time and energy to learn how to advocate more for positive differences within the profession. Such advocacy ought to be based on critical self-reflection and collaborative critical appraisal of our practices in light of research and literature (Woodrow & Fasoli, 1998).

Advocacy happens at various levels from individual, to organization, and then to wider society. Beginning at the program level we have significant opportunities to impact on our current and future directions. Linke (1999) encourages us to focus our advocacy on and for the rights of children through modelling our commitment to their voices within our programs and our communities. At the society level we are faced with greater challenges as political, social, and cultural structures are more difficult to influence. However, by using collective advocacy strategies that focus on these larger structures, it is more likely that we can influence directions for the common good. As a way of actioning this, Sharp (1999) beckons us to participate at the policy development level of government through communication, media, and legal strategies.

Think deeply about your values and beliefs. Reflection and communication are focal strategies in helping you relate to others about these beliefs. Act upon your deepened understandings and take responsibility for becoming active in political, professional, and scholarly webs of influence (Meade, 1995 cited in Rodd, 1997). Take these activities beyond this article and implement them in your real world.

References

Australian Early Childhood Association (1990). *Code of Ethics*. Watson, ACT: Australian Early Childhood Association.

Feeney, S., & Freeman, N. K. (1999). *Ethics and the Early Childhood Educator: Using the NAEYC Code*. Washington, DC: National Association for the Education of Young Children.

Fulwiler, T. (1987). *The Journal Book*. Portsmouth: Heinemann.

Limerick, D., & Cunnington, B. (1993). *Managing the New Organisation: a blueprint for networks and strategic alliances*. Chatswood, Australia: Business & Professional Publishing.

Linke, P. (1999). "Advocacy and Children's Services." *Rattler*, Spring, no. 49, 2-4.

Activities to promote advocacy:

1. One way of influencing at the program level is to advocate publicly through posters. In groups of two or three, design an effective poster for informing parents about a current issue at your center. When you are planning a poster for use with adults or children, there are key design principles (taken from the marketing and/or advertising world) that help you communicate messages more effectively. These include such hints as:

   - being clear about your purpose;
   - incorporating clear rather than messy layouts;
   - limiting the number of fonts;
   - ensuring permission is gained for all photographs; and
   - presenting children in natural and non-objectified positions.

   - providing plenty of empty space;
   - using print that is very large and easily read;
   - breaking up written text with illustrations or photographs;

2. At the society level we can advocate publicly through various forms of media, such as newspapers. As a whole group, brainstorm various topics that you believe early childhood educators should influence. In small groups, select one of these topics and write a one page newspaper article that would give voice to the profession within the wider society.

3. Becoming an active member of a professional early childhood education organization is one way of influencing government policy. As a small group, identify a common issue that you believe ought to be raised at government level. Next, identify early childhood education professional organizations that group members are affiliated with. Share what you know about the current advocacy processes of these organizations.

   Now consider how you can put your identified issue on the agenda of one of these organizations. What role can you take in driving a campaign about your issue? What suggestions can you make to the organization about the kind of campaign that you would like to be part of? Draft a letter requesting the issue be raised within the organization and outline your key ideas for the campaign. Return to the whole workshop group and share your lists of organizations and your campaign letter.

McCrea, N. (May 2000). Leaders as Navigators of Early Childhood Education: Mapping Organisations and Steering Others, paper presented to the World Forum on Early Care and Education, Singapore.

Morrison, D. (1994). Professional Learning as Personal Experience, *Early Childhood Education, (27)*2, 31-37.

Morrison, G. (1997). *Fundamentals of Early Childhood Education*. Upper Saddle River, NJ: Prentice-Hall.

Rodd, J. (1997). Learning to Develop as Early Childhood Professionals, *Australian Journal of Early Childhood, (22)*1, 1-5.

Sharp, C. (Spring 1999). Systems Advocacy in a Changing Political Climate, *Rattler*, no. 49, 5-7.

Waters, J. (1998). *Helping Young Children Understand Their Rights*. Melbourne, Australia: The World Organisation of Early Childhood Education.

Woodrow, C., & Fasoli, L. (1998). Change and Criticism: Thinking Critically in Early Childhood Collaboration, *Australian Journal of Early Childhood, (23)*1, 40-44.

Rhonda Forrest is a lecturer in early childhood education at the University of New England, Armidale, New South Wales, Australia. She researches and teaches in leadership and professionalism with a particular interest in beginning directors. Contact her at rforrest@metz.une.edu.au.

Associate Professor Nadine McCrea, Ph.D., was the foundational program director of early childhood education at the University of New England (1998-2001) (visit: http://fehps.une.edu.au/f/d/edu/Earlychildhood/earlych.html). She is currently associate dean (Teaching and Learning) on the Faculty of Education, Health, and Professional Studies. She has taught and written widely about the socialness of food, leadership, and professionalism in early childhood. Contact her at nmccrea@metz.une.edu.au.

Using Beginnings Workshop to Train Teachers by Kay Albrecht

This One is a Slam Dunk!!: Forrest and McCrea make training on the topic of relating and sharing professionally easy by outlining two excellent activities, one for exploring team relationships and another for exploring advocacy. Try them out!! For information about mind mapping, see Joyce Wycoff's *MindMapping: your personal guide to exploring creativity and problem-solving* (1991, New York: Berkeley Books).

Caregiver Health and Safety

CAREGIVER HEALTH AND SAFETY

Taking Care of Caregivers: Wellness for Every Body

by Susan S. Aronson

Wellness is a state of mind and body: how you feel about sensations of normal body functions and how you choose to address the wear and tear of life. Wellness is the result of preventive health care and wise personal behaviors supported by science and common sense. For most people, promoting wellness involves making better choices among limited options. Few early childhood professionals have much time or resources to lavish on fitness.

Child care directors need to think about wellness because improving the health of adults who work in child care pays double dividends. It not only helps the individual, but also everyone who depends on them.

By using familiar planning skills, you can easily promote staff wellness. The approach is not unlike skillful planning for developmentally appropriate experiences of children in group care settings. Plan for activities that will meet predictable physical and mental health needs. Making time in staff meetings to engage caregivers in thinking about these issues will emphasize the value that the program places on caring for caregivers.

Rest

Planning for a wellness-promoting day begins the previous evening. Making the transition from a busy day to restful sleep is easier if you can dissipate the worries and stresses of the day. Pleasurable physical activity, writing, or talking about what happened are stress management tools. Selective TV viewing is fine, but should not take the place of physical activity, writing, or talking about what happened during the day. When the weather is nice in the evening, taking a walk with a companion is an especially desirable and healthy activity. The combination of walking and talking helps resolve unfinished business still churning in your brain from the events of the day.

Aim for bed at a time that offers the possibility of seven or eight unbroken hours of sleep after an hour or so of wind-down time. If you keep doing one chore after another until you drop, restful sleep is unlikely. Remarkably, some of the most urgent work that you feel you must do in the evening has to be redone or becomes irrelevant after a week or so. If the task matters, sharing the work with others or scheduling expectations at realistic levels makes sense.

Late nights on weekends are counterproductive, too. Disciplined rest routines, not irregular late nights and catch up late mornings, keep body rhythms humming along at their best. When exceptions occur, notice the way you feel for the next few days — it is your body telling you that staying up late wasn't a good idea.

Plan for mini-rest breaks during the day. Your workday may consist of talking on the telephone, working at desks and countertops, meeting with parents and staff while standing in corridors, and bending to be at child-eye-level. The work of child care providers is physically demanding and often stressful. Both wellness and work quality improve with disciplined scheduling of a few breaks to go outside, use the restroom, or do a five minute restoration exercise or meditation.

Exercise, muscle stretching, healthy eating during the day, and good bedtime snack choices are all related to stress management and more restful sleep. Read the articles in this issue of *Exchange* that focus on musculoskeletal fitness, mental health, and nutrition — then incorporate as many of these healthy practices as you can.

Arrange your environment for healthy living. Install sound absorbing materials wherever you can to reduce noise levels. Provide a comfortable temperature (65 to 75 degrees F) and relative humidity (30-50%) where you work and sleep. Reduce the use of unnecessary chemicals in the environment, especially those that have fumes and those known to be toxic. Limit your use of medications and chemicals to those that are more likely to help than harm your body.

Daytime body routines

Start by looking at what you typically do from the moment you get up. Do you eat breakfast, literally the meal that breaks the fast and fuels the beginning of your day? Take a lesson from the research that shows most kids don't do as well at school in the morning if they skip breakfast. After breakfast, do you brush your teeth? Do you floss daily? The bacteria that get into the blood stream from lack of good oral hygiene can harm the cardiovascular system.

Do you take time to sit on the toilet and have a bowel movement when you first feel the urge, or are you so rushed that you suppress it? Typically, bowel activity is stimulated by the increased activity and eating that occurs after you get out of bed and have breakfast. Hurried morning preparations and post-mealtime rushing off to other activities sometimes interferes with these routines. The result is altered body functions that can lead to disease.

Motor vehicle and pedestrian safety

On the way to work, many people put haste ahead of safe choices as they handle the challenges of vehicular and pedestrian travel. The leading cause of death for people up to their mid-30s is motor vehicle-related injuries. In fact, transportation injury remains a key contributor to death and disability throughout life. It's great to walk whenever you can for exercise and fresh air. Be sure to cross the street where you would want a child to cross to be safe. When you travel in a car, always buckle up, no matter how distracted or late you are. How do you drive? Do you roll through stop signs? Do you exceed the speed limit by more than 5 mph? These behaviors are associated with higher risk of premature death. Use self-talk to give yourself the advice you would give to children in your care so they avoid taking unacceptable risks. Make good habits habitual, rather than exceptional.

Hand washing

Preventing infection through effective hand washing is much neglected. Watch how often people fail to wash before eating. How often do you see adults and children pick their noses, bite their nails or cuticles, and then touch all the surfaces around them? Studies in public restrooms show that around half of the users don't wash after using the toilet. Since so many surfaces we touch have germs on them, keep your own hands away from your food and your mouth until you wash them.

Adults benefit from routine health examinations

Health examinations for adults working in the child care setting are a great opportunity to reflect on current health-related habits that could be improved. If your own clinician doesn't use some type of questionnaire to assess health behaviors, use one of the on-line self-assessments from the Internet. Type in "wellness" as a search term on the government sponsored website www.Healthfinder.gov to identify reliable Internet sources of health information and self-assessment tools.

Honest use of a self-assessment provides a baseline for discussions with a doctor about what to do to improve health. Hearing and vision screenings are relevant to child care job performance, too. Good clinicians combine an insightful discussion of what their patients say about their health with physical examination and laboratory findings to recommend what to do for personal wellness.

Health insurance is especially critical to child care workers because of the increased risk of infectious disease and injury inherent in caring for groups of young children. Moreover, if child care workers do contract infectious disease or suffer injury, they may put children at risk. Reflecting these realities, the soon-to-be published 2nd edition of *Caring for Our Children, the national health and safety performance standards for out-of-home child care,* require that all paid and volunteer staff members who work more than 40 hours per month have a health appraisal before their first involvement in child care work and every two years (or less) thereafter. These national standards and separate recommendations of the Centers for Disease Control and Prevention (CDC) also require that all child care workers have regular assessments of their need for updated immunization against vaccine-preventable infectious diseases. In addition, OSHA requires hepatitis B vaccine for child care workers who have blood exposure while providing ordinary first aid.

Occupational risks for infection in the child care setting

Prevention strategies for adults include routine immunizations. In addition to needing boosters for tetanus and diphtheria protection every decade, adults who work in child care should check with their doctors to be sure they are already immune or have received vaccines for measles, mumps, rubella, varicella (chicken pox), polio, and hepatitis B.

Other vaccines are appropriate for child care providers. All adults who work in child care should seek influenza vaccine on an annual basis. Recent reports link the community spread of influenza to exposure to group care settings for children. Those who are 65 years of age or older (e.g. foster grandparents) need pneumococcal vaccine, too. In some communities where the rates of hepatitis A are high, the Centers for Disease Control and Prevention recommend that the entire child care workforce should have hepatitis A vaccine. Check with local public health authorities to see if you work in such a community.

Those who work in child care settings are exposed to common infectious diseases. Exclusion for infectious diseases for adults follows the same rules as those for children. If you are too sick to participate normally in the program, you shouldn't be there. Taking a day off may be tough if there are few substitutes. Sometimes adults report to work when they are too ill because they believe it is the noble thing to do. Taking a day off to recover from a minor illness may avoid many days of lingering symptoms that reduce adult performance. Supervisors should remind ill adults in child care that their responsibility is not to be a hero by coming to work when sick, but to do what is necessary to get well and function effectively.

Having more colds than usual during the first year of working in child care is typical. If the cold lingers on for more than ten days, a visit to a clinician is in order. Secondary complications may require treatment. Ignoring these symptoms saps energy and increases vulnerability to the next infection that comes along.

The increased exposure to infectious disease agents in group care can pose special problems for the fetus of a woman who is not already immune. Many women who work in child care are of childbearing age. Many become pregnant during the period of their child care employment. Women of childbearing age should discuss their risks with their clinicians. While most adults are already immune to these diseases, those who might become pregnant should discuss their own status with their obstetricians. Blood tests can be done to tell if a particular woman is already immune or at risk during her pregnancy. Scrupulous hand washing helps prevent the spread of many infections. The diseases of greatest concern for a woman who may become pregnant while working in child care are: chickenpox, cytomegalovirus, Fifth Disease, and rubella.

Guidelines for testing the child care workforce have changed recently. The 2nd edition of *Caring for Our Children* will describe a new approach to TB screening. Adults in early childhood settings need only an initial skin testing for tuberculosis when they first begin working in child care, and thereafter have further evaluations based on their own clinician's assessment of what should be done. Routine TB skin tests every two years are no longer recommended. The most important way TB is spread is by contact with someone who has active tuberculosis and has symptoms of illness. Prompt testing of contacts of someone who has TB, not routine screening of people without symptoms, controls the spread of this disease.

Adult health matters to the quality of child care

Directors have a legitimate interest in the health status of adults who work in the child care setting. Quality child care requires consistently supportive human relationships. When caregivers and supervisors are ill, relationships and performance suffer. So plan for wellness of adults in child care as a component of quality care for children.

Susan S. Aronson, MD, FAAP, is clinical professor of pediatrics at the University of Pennsylvania and a pediatrician in Philadelphia, Pennsylvania.

Using Beginnings Workshop to Train Teachers by Kay Albrecht

Health Assessment: To get a school-wide view of the health status, use Aronson's article as a beginning activity. This article is full of good examples of what we should be doing to maintain wellness. Take each suggestion (for example, gets 7-8 hours of sleep; or exercises every day) and ask teachers to arrange themselves in order on a continuum. In figuring out their place on the continuum (do I get more sleep than the person next to me, or less; or do I exercise more, or less), teachers will uncover the personal areas of wellness that could be improved. Directors will see if they have a BIG wellness challenge (if everyone bunches up at the less than 7-8 hours of sleep end of the continuum) or a little wellness challenge (if most teachers are on the gets exercise everyday end of the continuum).

Formal Health Self-Assessment: Post the web page mentioned in the article by the computer used by teachers. Encourage them to go on-line, find an assessment tool, complete it, and take the results to their physician during annual physicals.

Simple Supports: Add dental floss to the teacher's first aid kit (you know, the one that has over the counter medications like ibuprofen, Tylenol, etc. in it that help teachers stay at work!) Consider adding lockers to the teachers' bathroom so that teachers can keep toothbrushes and other personal care items handy.

Insurance Realities: Consider the recommendation to provide health insurance seriously. If your school doesn't provide it now, appoint a study group to investigate how insurance might be added and the impact the addition would have on the center. Make sure to appoint some parents to the study group so that they can share with other parents what they find. Make a plan to provide health insurance — even if the plan is a long term, strategic one.

Handwashing Routines: Add staff training on handwashing to your annual training calendar. Find ways to make it fun and creative. For example, brainstorm songs to sing during handwashing to make sure adults and children wash fronts and backs of their hands and in-between their fingers; fingerplays to say while handwashing that keep adults and children washing long enough to get rid of germs; make creative signs and reminders to post near sinks (maybe using children's art to make the point!); have a guest speaker from a hospital come to share strategies used in medical settings, etc. This is an important recurring training need that should not be overlooked.

Sick Policies and Procedures: Aronson hits a nerve when she talks about needing to come to work sick or well. Many times teachers are faced with this dilemma. Get teachers to write a tip sheet for deciding if they are too ill to come to school. Experienced teachers can share their wellness strategies — like how they get extra rest when they feel a cold coming on, as well as how they decide when they are too sick to come to school. Include tips about deciding when to see a doctor and when to wait it out; when to take medicine and when not to; home remedies that seem to work, etc. After the tip sheet is developed, have your consulting physician review it to see if the folk knowledge of the school is medically valid. Add the tip sheet to your staff manual.

CAREGIVER HEALTH AND SAFETY

Caregiver Mental Health

by Susan S. Aronson

Child care is challenging work, physically and mentally. The science of early brain development emphasizes the key role caregivers play in providing warm, responsive care for children. Not only is child care labor-intensive, it is highly interactive — both on the adult-child and adult-adult level. Staff interact with other staff, parents, and with members of the larger community on a daily basis.

All the public and professional attention focused on the problems of quality in child care puts everyone who works in this field on the defensive. Competent caregivers are in a constant state of alert to meet the needs of children — ready to restructure the environment and social situations to maintain positive experiences for children. As all workers do, caregivers come to the job with personal life concerns. Nobody parks their worries at the door when they leave home. Navigating through the day takes a lot of skill and energy.

During the usual work day in child care, directors and caregivers are expected to do more than care for children. They support parents and co-workers, too. Parents often seek support from child care staff. Many parents find their multi-tasking lives barely manageable. Some are hungry for emotional support both for their children and for themselves.

In addition to having little time for breaks and a high intellectual demand, child care staff have few opportunities for private quiet moments during the work day. Separate, private, and comfortable break areas for adults who work in child care facilities is hard to find in many centers. Even restrooms may be communal spaces.

Mental health and emotional well-being are key issues to keeping child care staff on the job and doing well. In the past few years, the mind-body interface has become a mainstream health concept. Although there are no published studies to prove it, workplace stress in child care probably plays a key role in causing physical illness. So what can directors do to care for the mental health of child care staff?

Tune in to stress. Stress is a natural part of life that motivates activity — some of which is desirable. When stress is not managed well, it causes strain and discomfort — expressed physiologically and mentally. Signs of poorly managed stress include inability to concentrate, inexplicable sadness, difficulty sleeping, fatigue even when sleep hours are sufficient, irritability, loss of appetite, and self-medicating behaviors with alcohol, caffeine, and other drugs. Physical signs of stress include headaches, pain or discomfort in the back, neck, and stomach.

Promote mutual support. Urge all adults involved in child care to seek and offer support to one another in staff meetings, informal support groups, friendships, staff retreats, sharing of information about commnity resources and ways to get responsible help from Internet resources. Child care is an extended family, not only for the parents and children who use the services, but also for the adults who provide the services. Being alert to the needs of others is empowering. While sharing the details of personal life stresses with peers and supervisors may be inappropriate, letting others know that you are stressed is rarely news to them. Make sure that stressed adults have someone with whom they can talk about the nature of personal problems. We all need to share our thinking to gain insight and move from anxiety to problem-solving. This level of support may not be appropriate for on-the-job relationships, but colleagues can check that those who seem unusually stressed have and are using such relationships with friends and family or seeking professional help.

Promote pleasurable and stress-relieving physical activity. Even five minutes of a fun activity can leave you feeling much better. Physical activity is relaxing and releases hormones that self-medicate in a healthy way. Simple stress-relieving activities do not necessarily require much skill, space, time, or equipment.

For example, a few minutes of scarf-juggling gets your upper body muscles stretched, and switches your mind for a few moments onto doing something that is fun and easy to do.

Juggling scarves can be purchased in bulk with easy instructions from Laughter Works, 34125 CR 352, Decatur, MI 49045, phone (616) 624-9044. Bulk-purchased nylon juggling scarves can be packaged in closable sandwich bags so directors, staff, and parents can each have a set to learn scarf juggling at a meeting, then carry around in a pocket to use for quick relaxation breaks.

Scarf juggling is one of a variety of relaxation exercises that require little space and time. You can do stretching and relaxing of muscle groups without leaving what you are doing. It's easy to do — and very young children can learn to do it with you. Focus on stretching from the top down, bottom up or extremity-to-extremity. Using imaging techniques that actually lower your pulse and blood pressure takes less than a minute. Quick and easy stretching exercises, imaging, scarf juggling, and other relaxation activities can make you feel much better in the middle of a busy day.

Find time to have fun with whatever you are doing. Children are always doing something that can bring a smile, even a good laugh. Laughter is good medicine. When we laugh, we release internal chemicals that make us feel good all over. Laughter is a natural tension reducer and appropriate if it is not at someone else's expense.

Enjoy the value of early care and education to the future of society. Working in child care is a demanding and usually poorly paid occupation. The fact is that a huge part of the compensation is the knowledge that what you are doing is meaningful to others. Early care and education makes a difference in the lives of many children and their families. Know your work matters, that you are important to children and families. Talking about it with peers and those who are less informed is good for you and good for child care.

Susan S. Aronson, MD, FAAP, is clinical professor of pediatrics at the University of Pennsylvania and a pediatrician in Philadelphia, Pennsylvania.

Using Beginnings Workshop to Train Teachers by Kay Albrecht

Staff Meeting Problem-Solving: At a staff meeting, make two lists of problems that cause anxiety for teachers — one personal list and one professional list. Take one or two examples and try Aronson's idea of moving from the problem to problem-solving. Brainstorm ways the school can help and ways colleagues can help. When teachers see that problem-solving does work (at least some of the time), they will be more willing to get out of their bad spot and look for some solutions. Alert directors will take the list of anxiety-causing problems at school and see if there is anything they can do to address some of them. Really alert directors will have a list of what bothers whom to incorporate into her management plan for responding to teachers when they are stressed. Amazing directors will pair problem-solving ideas with their creator and help him apply his ideas when anxiety strikes.

Take a Walk!: Start a "Take a Walk Break Program" for teachers. Use extra down time of floaters or substitutes to give teachers ten minute walking breaks once or twice a day. Make it fun by identifying walks of different distances with mileposts (perhaps made by the children in woodworking). Keep a record of those that walk and give them recognition at a staff meeting as a subtle encouragement for others to add exercise to their daily routine. If you can't do it daily, try once a week. If you don't have the staff to do it, look for alternatives like filling in yourself (what a great way to keep in touch with children and to show teachers you value good mental health and exercise), see if parents might provide support for such a project, or identify volunteers who might be able to help.

Juggling Scarves: Order the juggling scarves that Aronson describes and introduce them at a staff meeting. Then, appoint a scarf supporter to find times during the day to add a little stretching fun to teachers' lives. At the staff meeting, discuss other relaxation ideas that teachers use and have them demonstrate them for their colleagues. See if any of their ideas could be incorporated into the mental health plan at your center.

CAREGIVER HEALTH AND SAFETY

Show and Tell: Modeling Healthy Behaviors and Attitudes

by Donna Rafanello

A teacher recently described herself to me as a *performer*. "Each morning," she said, "I dress the part and take the stage. If my performance is not good, the children know it. I have to be *up* for them and give them all I have."

My own experience in parenting my three-year-old daughter teaches me the same thing. In wanting to be a good example to her, I have changed the way I live my life. I eat more fruits and vegetables, cut back on sweets, and get a good night's rest. I know she's watching me, and I want her to learn by my example how to live a healthy life.

Children mimic us. Many of the funny stories we tell are based on observations of children who echo our words and imitate our behavior in their play. These can be quite comical. We learn from these observations that modeling is an effective way to shape children's behavior. When parents and other caregivers model healthy behavior and attitudes, we take care of ourselves and teach children the principles for healthy living.

Teacher as healthy role model

Teaching young children is emotionally and physically demanding work that requires the energy that comes with living a healthy lifestyle. Those of us who care for young children owe it to ourselves to be in good health, and we owe it to the children in our care. With young children watching us as closely as they do, it is essential that we recognize the role our own behavior plays in helping them establish their own healthy habits. "Walk the talk" and "Practice what you preach" and children will benefit from it. Helping children to value health and wellness contributes to their overall well-being now and throughout their lives. *Caring for Our Children* (American Public Health Association, APHA, and the American Academy of Pediatrics, AAP, 1992) defines health and safety standards for early childhood programs in the following way:

"For young children, health and education are inseparable . . . Education to promote healthy behaviors should be integrated wherever opportunities for learning occur. Health education should be seen not as a structured curriculum but as a daily component of the planned program that is part of child development. Health education shall include physical, oral, mental, and social health and shall be integrated daily in the program of activities" (p. 61).

Try this: Make a list of the important health habits that you and your staff feel children should demonstrate. Then identify when and where teachers can model these habits for children.

What teachers can do

Teachers have a unique and powerful role in influencing children's understanding of their bodies and in demonstrating the habits that contribute to overall good health. Here are five steps teachers can take to become positive role models for children.

Step 1: Build strong bodies

Eat well. This includes a variety of nutritious foods. Minimize your intake of caffeine, sugar, and fatty foods. Model good eating practices by sitting with children at mealtime and eating the foods that they are served. Have a relaxing lunch with pleasant conversation, including a discussion of the foods being served and how they build strong bodies.

Schedule a period of physical activity every day in addition to participating in activities with the children that contribute to your physical fitness.

Avoid drugs, alcohol, tobacco, and other toxic substances. Self-medicating with substances is a sign of poorly managed stress.

Adults' attitudes and behavior toward substance abuse are communicated to young children in numerous ways that affect their perception of what is acceptable. Smelling of cigarette smoke when you return from your break or talking with coworkers about your alcohol consumption sends powerful messages.

Recent media attention has focused on childhood obesity as a public health epidemic. According to Susan Aronson, M.D. (Dr. Sue), "Being overweight is unhealthy for children and adults. Many overweight young children become overweight adults. What children observe and do with adults sets lifetime expectations for activity and eating. Obesity raises the risk of illness in later childhood and in adult life. The list of diseases associated with obesity includes high blood pressure; high cholesterol; diabetes; heart disease and stroke; breast, prostate, and colon cancers; and others" (p. 30).

Try this: Consider establishing a health and wellness program with your staff like the one created by Bright Horizons Family Solutions. The "Be Fit BFAM" initiative motivated employees company-wide to make healthy changes to their lifestyle.

Step 2: Reduce the risk of injury

Wear shoes that protect your feet and don't interfere with Clogs, open-toe sandals, and high-heeled or platform shoes should not be worn. Purchase shoes with good shock-absorption or use shoe inserts for this purpose. Clothes that allow for movement and that are professional in appearance are also important. Tight or revealing clothing, long skirts, tank tops, and short skirts or shorts are discouraged.

Avoid dangling jewelry (earrings, bracelets, necklaces) that can present safety hazards to yourself and children.

Arrange classrooms to eliminate environmental obstacles and remove dangerous or broken equipment, furniture, and toys immediately to prevent injury.

Children will imitate this behavior to tragic consequences.

Try this: Consider the ways in which we send double messages to children. When we discourage children from wearing shoes, clothing, or jewelry that pose safety hazards, interfere with active play or appropriate hygiene and then wear these ourselves, we send mixed messages that interfere with their learning. When caregivers skip lunch, eat "fast foods," or drink soda and coffee in front f children, children see and learn from our behavior.

Step 3: Control infection

Demonstrate to children that you know how to take care of yourself by taking time off from work to rest and recuperate at home. Do your part to prevent the spread of illness.

Wash your hands often, especially after wiping your own or children's noses, toileting, handling animals or animal waste, cleaning up messes, and before handling food. Handwashing is the single most effective method of disease prevention. Germs are harder to remove from hands with painted and artificial fingernails or jewelry, so avoid using these adornments at work.

Try this: Discuss your center's sick policy and the ways in which it encourages or discourages staff from taking time off when they are ill.

Step 4: Foster emotional health

Manage your stress level. Caring for young children is emotionally and physically demanding work. Recognize stress-related symptoms like tension headaches, neck and shoulder strain, irritability, digestive troubles, and frequent illness. Learn new strategies for managing time, space, and people (Jorde-Bloom, 1982). In this area, as with others, the focus is on prevention. Anger directed at children and physical abuse are more likely to occur when caregivers are experiencing high stress (APHA & AAP, 1992).

Develop coping skills to help you manage job-related stress. Talking about stress with young children helps them learn to manage their feelings in healthy ways and to use play to reduce anxiety (APHA & AAP, 1992). Children learn what they live. When we demonstrate healthy ways of dealing with anger, sadness, envy, and other emotions, we teach children positive alternatives to negative behaviors and violence.

Ask for help when you need it. Social support, according to the authors of *Caring for Our Children*, is one of the chief ways we build self-esteem.

Try this: Implement rules in your program that help staff manage stress. Here are a few to consider:
1) Don't gossip;
2) Use humor to defuse tense situations;
3) Create support systems among staff including team leaders, mentors, or buddies that diminish feelings of isolation; and
4) Respect teachers' break times.

Step 5: Demonstrate self-care

Take pride in your appearance. When we look good, we feel good. Feelings of self-respect and self-esteem positively affect those around us.

Maintain clean hair, clothes, teeth, skin, and fingernails. These efforts will help you feel good and keep you healthier longer.

Try this: Discuss personal appearance as a reflection of self-esteem. Support each other in your efforts to be the best you can be.

The director's role

Paula Jorde Bloom's research on organizational climate (Bloom, 1997) has shown that directors set the tone for what goes on in their programs. In this area of health maintenance and promotion the same is true. Here are some ways that directors encourage their staff to make health and wellness a priority:

■ Foster a nurturing, caring environment where all people treat each other with respect and caring, and speak gently to each other;

■ Have a plan in place to ensure adequate supervision of the children when a caregiver needs to take a sick or mental health day;

■ Expect caregivers to take care of themselves and to ask for help when they need it;

■ Include topics like stress management and health practices on the agenda at staff meetings. Consider bringing in outside speakers to facilitate these discussions;

■ Anticipate stressful times of the year and be proactive in your planning;

■ Set the tone for your program by being positive and hopeful about what is possible for your staff and your program. Projecting a positive attitude sets the stage for more positive interactions with others.

Remember that the children are watching you and learning by your example. Children learn more from what you do than from what you say. Contribute to their lifelong health by demonstrating healthy habits. You just might feel better, too!

References

American Public Health Association & American Academy of Pediatrics. (1992). *Caring for our children: National health and safety performance standards: Guidelines for out-of-home child care programs.* Washington, DC and Elk Grove Village, IL: APHA and AAP.

Aronson, S. (2000, July). Updates on healthy eating and walkers. *Exchange, 134,* 30.

Bloom, P. J. (1997). *A great place to work: Improving conditions for staff in young children's programs.* Washington, DC: NAEYC.

Jorde-Bloom, P. (1982). *Avoiding burnout: Strategies for managing time, space, and people in early childhood education.* Lake Forest, IL: New Horizons.

Donna Rafanello, M.Ed., is assistant professor of Child & Adult Development at Long Beach City College in Long Beach, California and coordinates Exchange's Mentor Writing Project. She can be reached by e-mail at dsrafanello@aol.com.

Using Beginnings Workshop to Train Teachers by Kay Albrecht

Rafanello makes it very easy for trainers to identify training ideas — she identifies them in each section and calls them "Try this." Look through these ideas to add to your training plan.

Assessment: Have each teacher conduct a healthy lifestyle assessment based on the ideas presented in the article. Have teachers rate themselves on a scale of 1 to 5 with 1 being doesn't describe me at all and 5 being describes me to a T. Add up the scores and have teachers reflect on their scores.

One, Two, Stretch, Again!: Adding exercise to an already busy day is always a challenge. Consider making a plan to provide exercise for teachers at the center on a weekly basis. Purchase a video and follow along. Go on a walk together. Join a gym that is nearby and convenient. These strategies will work better if management supports them and tries to make them happen.

Water, Water, Everywhere and Not a Soft Drink in Sight!: Place a thermos of cold water in strategic places throughout the school to support teachers in getting the water they need to stay healthy. Act on the suggestion to practice what we preach by limiting soft drink consumption in front of the children. To really make this idea a hit, get children to make glasses for their teachers, adding artwork that gives the container a flare and permanence that supports conservation.

Me, Too!: Create your own version of this industry leader's BFAM Wellness Program at your school. You can do it, too.

Take a Day Off — I Really Mean It!!: At a staff meeting, discuss your sick leave policy and the ways it encourages and discourages teachers from taking time off. Candidly discuss ways that teachers can feel better about taking time off when they need it and when management can provide time off and when it can't. These kinds of conversations are hard to have because directors often feel attacked by staff for circumstances beyond their control. Take the risk, but set up some guidelines for input like offering a solution when identifying a problem or roadblock to taking time off.

For Directors Only: Turn Rafanello's list of ways directors can support wellness into a self-evaluation. Rate yourself and develop an action plan to improve your response to supporting wellness. Try to identify the things you already do and then reflect on what else could be done. After you do a self-evaluation, consider asking teachers for their feedback to see if they evaluate your support in the same way you do. If they don't, work on finding ways to help teachers recognize what you do, as well as what you don't do.

CAREGIVER HEALTH AND SAFETY

Preventing Work-Related Musculoskeletal Injuries

by Alicia M. Wortman, edited by Susan S. Aronson

Common sense tells us that happy healthy employees are more productive in the workplace. In the child care environment, employee productivity directly affects our children. Although researchers have studied the health and epidemiology of illness among children in out-of-home day care, few have examined the occupational health of caregivers. Just like any workplace, there are environmental and occupational hazards in a child care center. Ideally, we want to minimize the hazards and maximize the opportunities to ensure the health and safety of the employees.

Ergonomics for child care

Ergonomics is the scientific study of fitting a job to an individual. This science can, and should, be applied to the child care setting. Musculoskeletal injuries are relatively high among child care providers. The Bureau of Labor Statistics reported that one of every 100 child care workers suffered a nonfatal occupational injury in 1999 (Bureau of Labor Statistics). Working as a child care provider can be a physically demanding job. It requires constant interaction with active (sometimes hyperactive), spontaneous, impulsive, heavy (sometimes very heavy) children. Lifting, stooping, bending, climbing, crawling, reaching, pulling, and pushing are just some of the strenuous activities required. According to the Center for Disease Control and Prevention, back injury is the most common cause of occupational injury for child care providers (U.S. Public Health Service). Aches, pains, muscle strains, and sprains are also commonplace. Many of these musculoskeletal injuries can be prevented.

Phyllis M. King noted the paucity of documented research regarding the health and safety of the child care provider in a child care setting (King, Gratz, Scheuer, & Claffey). However, research in other workplace settings can be applied to the child care setting. Child care providers need to be educated about

what to do, and what resources to use, so they can improve the efficiency and safety of their working environment. The medical literature reports that most back pain is not the result of a single injury. Even though pain may be felt suddenly, the problem is almost always due to a combination of several factors. These factors include: poor posture, faulty body mechanics, stressful living or work habits, loss of flexibility, and a general decline of physical fitness (Saunders). The good news is that we have control over these factors. We can improve our posture and body mechanics. We can work with our co-workers to improve the ergonomic set-up of our workplace. And, we can exercise regularly to improve our flexibility and general fitness.

Education is key

The child care provider must learn about these issues as part of employment orientation. However, the education should not stop here. Education of employees should be an ongoing process with regular in-service, provision of written brochures and literature, and reminders that help staff incorporate the behaviors into the daily routine. For instance, pictures of proper lifting techniques and written reminders posted on the wall.

Education on use of proper body mechanics must begin with a basic understanding of the anatomy and physiology of the spine. The spine is a unique set of joints which serve many vital functions. Not only does the spine serve as the foundation for our skeleton, providing us with both stability and mobility, but it also houses our spinal cord, which is an extension of our brain — receiving and providing sensorimotor input/output. The spine has a natural inward curve (or lordosis) in the lumbar and cervical spine and a natural outward (or kyphosis) in the thoracic spine. These curves exist to provide necessary shock absorption, stability, and mobility needed for normal bio-mechanical function. We must support and maintain these natural curvatures, or what has been termed as a *neutral spine*. Find your neutral spine by standing erect and gently tightening your abdominal (stomach) muscles. Perform this exercise in various positions: sitting, standing, and lying. With continued practice there will be carry-over to retrain these muscles to naturally support the lumbar spine without conscious effort.

The spine is not supported when you sit in a slumped position. This can be avoided by sitting with low-back support. If you must sit on the floor, sit against a wall or with a large *husband*-style pillow for your back. Adults should use adult furniture whenever possible. When the situation requires using child-sized chairs, tables, or desks, be sure to sit with as much back support as possible. Stand up as if rising from a squat position, keeping your back straight, pelvis level, and abdomen tight while you use your thigh muscles to raise your body to standing.

Getting to child level

Avoid leaning forward or downward to reach or assist children. Instead, assume a squatting position or kneeling position to bring your body closer to the children. Use small kneeling pads (similar to the type used for gardening) to allow more comfortable kneeling when working with children who are sitting at child-sized tables. Do not sit for prolonged periods of time. When you must sit, use comfortable chairs with back support (rockers, gliders, etc.).

Stretching

Break up bouts of sitting with gentle stretching exercises. When you sit, your spine naturally flexes (or rounds). It is important to counterbalance this with some gentle extension exercises. For instance, each time you rise from a seated position, place your hands in the small of your back and gently lean backward. Hold for a few seconds and return to the natural upright position. Repeat several times throughout the day. Another useful technique involves simply reaching your arms towards the ceiling, in order to stretch and extend the trunk and neck.

Standing

Proper posture should be used while standing as well. When standing for a prolonged period of time, shift your weight from side to side and change positions. Adjust the heights of changing tables so that the child you are changing is at your waist level. Use step stools for accessing high-to-reach places. Reorganize areas so that the most commonly used items are at an accessible level while standing.

A buddy system

If possible, install large mirrors (shatter-resistant, of course) throughout the child care center. This will help to provide constant reminders to improve your posture and body mechanics. Also, use a buddy system so co-workers remind each other when faulty body mechanics are observed.

Footwear

Be sure that you wear comfortable shoes with good shock-absorption. With every step, your foot must absorb one-and-a-half times your body weight. You can purchase over-the-counter shoe inserts to increase the shock-absorption of your shoe. This will help divert unnecessary stress to your weight-bearing joints. Avoid wearing high heels or hard-heeled shoes.

Lifting

Another way to reduce stress to the spine is by reducing the amount of lifting. This may be a difficult task in the child care environment. When lifting, use proper lifting techniques. Tighten your stomach musculature as you lift. This helps the muscles to provide a corset-like support to the spine. Bend at your knees and hips and bring the item or child close to your body before lifting. Do not twist or turn when lifting. Twisting stresses the muscles, ligaments, and joints of the spine complex.

Avoid repetitive lifting from the floor. Have the children pick up toys and other items from the floor. Incorporate this into daily clean-up time. Always lower the crib side before lifting the child out. Utilize a ramp or small, stable stepladders, or stairs to allow children, with close and continuous supervision, to climb up to changing tables or other places to which they would ordinarily be lifted. Use convenient equipment, like a multi-seat stroller, for moving children, reducing the necessity for carrying them long distances.

Exercise

Finally, incorporate exercise into daily routines. Maintaining general fitness and flexibility is essential to maintaining musculoskeletal health. Incorporating some of the gentle stretches mentioned above is a good way of ensuring that you maintain your flexibility. Institute walking programs and other fitness programs for the staff to encourage overall physical fitness. Work together as a team by developing an ergonomics mission statement that supports the mission of the organization. For example: "The mission of the XYZ Ergonomics Program is to support quality child care through the safe and innovative use of ergonomics, maximizing productivity, and protecting the health of the workforce" (Worrell). Use a team approach to develop ideas to improve the ergonomics of your child care center.

Wise Moves

Challenge	Wise Moves
Lifting children, toys, supplies	Avoid lifting by having children climb steps with help. Pull child or object to be lifted as close as possible directly in front of you; squat and wrap your arms around whatever you are lifting. Then tighten stomach muscles and use thigh muscles to raise yourself and your load. Lower objects and children by sliding them down your body to the level where you can squat or kneel to lower whatever you are putting down to its a destination.
Inadequate work heights	Reorganize to store frequently used objects where you can reach them easily. Store heavy objects at waist height so you don't have to lift them. Adjust diapering and similar work surfaces to waist height; use adult-sized chairs whenever you can; squat or kneel on a kneepad if you can't sit down next to children to help. Use step stools to reach high places.
Lifting infants in and out of cribs	Do not use cribs with floor level mattresses or those that do not have a side you can drop when putting children in or out. Get you and the child as close to the crib side as possible before you lift.
Frequent sitting on the floor without back support	When possible, sit against a wall or furniture that supports your back. Sit with a little pillow in the small of your back when you can. Stretch when you get up.
Carrying heavy objects or children	Use carts and strollers. Let children climb up with a step stool. If possible, divide heavy loads into several smaller loads and use carts that can be slid under the load and then tilt the load onto the cart.
Awkward posture to open windows or adjust objects	Move objects away from the window to get as close as possible to it. Put one foot on a step stool for better leverage. Lubricate the window mecha nism to make opening it easier. Ask for help from a co-worker when the job is hard.
Sweeping/picking up crumbs and small toys from the floor	Use a long-handled dustpan and broom. Keep a separate clean one for toys and one for things going into the trash.
Caring for children with special needs	Get specific training from the child's physical therapist about how to move and carry the child.
Caring for children during active play when sudden moves may be needed	Avoid twisting. Practice turning and bending to intercept a running or falling child so the move becomes natural. Bend knees when pushing children in swings. Use good body mechanics to help children on and off equipment.

Source: Work, 6:25-32: The ergonomics of child care: conducting worksite analyses (King, Gratz, Scheuer, & Claffey).

References

Bureau of Labor Statistics. (December 2000). U.S. Department of Labor.

U.S. Public Health Service. (1996). *The ABCs of safe and healthy child care: a handbook for child care providers.*

King, P. M., Gratz, R., Scheuer, G., & Claffey, A. (1996). The ergonomics of child care: conducting worksite analyses. *Work*, 6:25-32.

Saunders, H. (1992). *Self help manual: for your back.* Chaska, MN: Saunders Group, 6.

Worrell, G. (2001). Revitalizing your ergonomics program. *Occupational Health & Safety*, 70:93-4,7.

Alicia M. Wortman, MPT, is a physical therapist at the Hospital of the University of Pennsylvania in Philadelphia, Pennsylvania.

Using Beginnings Workshop to Train Teachers by Kay Albrecht

Practice Makes Perfect: Find a way to practice the proper body mechanics that Wortman recommends.

Adult Furniture? NOT!: Few classrooms have the adult-size furniture that is recommended in this article. At a staff meeting, identify which kind of adult-size furniture each classroom would like to have. Then brainstorm ways that it might be located and provided. Look to parents for support and ideas. They may have the solution in their garages or storage units right now. If not, make plans to add the furniture to your budget for next year — don't put it off — this one deserves your attention. Pay attention to durability and cleanability. You don't want to add someone else's discards to your classrooms. Teachers deserve to have functional and attractive equipment — it will improve their mental health!

Kneepads for Teachers: Purchase a pair of knee pads for teachers to use in the classroom. Present these small gifts as recognition of the many times a day a teacher literally gets down on her knees!

Ergonomics: Few of us really think about the issues raised by this author. Consider raising awareness and improving ergonomics by having an expert talk to teachers about what ergonomics is and how it might apply to the classroom teaching role. Appoint a small group of interested teachers to write an ergonomics mission statement (or use Wortman's) for your school and add it to the teacher training manual. Brainstorm ideas for meeting the mission statement.

CAREGIVER HEALTH AND SAFETY

It Is
No Small Thing

by Lilli-ann Buffin

Many years ago while shopping for a baby gift, I was scanning the gift cards when I came upon one with this lovely quote from Dickens, "It is no small thing that they, who are so fresh from God, love us." I snapped it up in an instant. While the card is no longer with me, the words form my daily mantra. This quote so beautifully describes my own commitment to a life with children. It *is* no small thing that children love us, and it *is* no small thing to care for children all day, every day.

As I meet more and more child care professionals around the country, I become increasingly aware that many of us feel a dissonance between politically correct statements about child care in our society and our actual experiences with child care on the front lines. We hear the public rhetoric about the importance of children, but the rhetoric does not match the very stressful reality we face in the day-to-day conditions of our work. Burnout is the special kind of stress that comes from the conditions of our work, and burned out describes our own transformation from idealistic to disillusioned. Here are some of the comments I hear from my colleagues that reflect the hurt and disillusionment they somtimes feel inside:

"I am all used up at the end of the day, so much so that I have little left to care for my own children. I feel terrible about that. How can I care for other people's children all day and have nothing left for my own?"

"I'm tired of being taken for granted by parents and society. It hurts when I hear parents say, 'I wish I could stay and play all day,' as though I am not working as hard or doing something as important as they are. And here I am, caring for their children."

"Children's behaviors are increasingly difficult and out of control. I feel I can't really enjoy my time with the children and, too often, there is little or no support from parents. Sometimes the parents even blame me or my center."

"The turnover is so great that it has become a full time job to interview and hire people. I have little time left to do the many other jobs required of a director. I spend too much time interviewing and substituting in the kitchen and the classroom."

"I love my job with the children, but I have to pay rent and have medical benefits. I can get better pay and benefits at the local fast food restaurant or discount department store and those jobs are less stressful."

Sometimes we are embarrassed by our negative feelings because we know child care is important work. Occasionally we feel guilty for wanting more for ourselves in money, recognition, and status. Often we feel anger and resentment that our wages and benefits limit our ability to attract and retain fine child care workers. Caring for children is hard work in a difficult social context but it cannot become an excuse for failing to take care of ourselves.

There are many excellent ideas contained in this issue for caring for our physical and mental health though it is all too easy to become cynical about all the *shoulds* and *oughts*. Often, the *shoulds* seem like the fairy tale version of life in child care. *Stay home when we are sick? Take our breaks? Drink water throughout the day? (And run the risk of having to use the bathroom, too?)*

Too many of us have come to believe that proper self-care is not achievable. We put the needs of others ahead of our own and pay a heavy price for doing so. We cannot let our negative feelings and experiences hinder us from taking charge of our personal well-being. We cannot continue to do what we have always done and expect to get different results.

Many years ago, psychologist Abraham Maslow identified five major categories of needs that motivate our behavior. Maslow's work is discussed and applied to work settings by Manning and

Curtis in *Human Behavior: Why People Do What They Do*. The five categories, in ascending order, are: (1) *survival needs* such as health, nutrition, exercise, rest, and shelter; (2) *security needs* such as medical insurance, retirement benefits, savings, and safe, stable work environments; (3) *love or affiliation needs* such as belonging to and feeling accepted in a group; (4) *respect needs* such as being considered worthwhile by others; and (5) *fulfillment needs*, the need to express our strong personal values and fulfill ourselves through our work.

How can we blend the knowledge we have about the true conditions of our work with the excellent self-care advice presented in this issue of *Exchange?* How can we address our personal needs and desires while still providing quality environments for children?

First, identify your own needs in each area. Again, this *Beginnings Workshop* provides many specific suggestions to improve and protect your well being. You can share this information with your center's director, owner, and others with whom you work. Second, individually and as a group, brainstorm ideas for identifying and meeting the needs of staff. Below are some questions to get this important discussion started:

Survival needs

Have you made a commitment to try some of the suggestions given in this issue for health, nutrition, exercise, rest, and stress management? Can you make better use of your center's physical space? Do you have adequate parking, restroom, and eating areas? Are you employing proper body mechanics in the physical aspects of your job? Is there opportunity in the day to go somewhere quiet to reflect and restore yourself? As an administrator, do you work individually and together with your staff to make your shared environment safer and more comfortable?

Security needs

Does your organization provide health and other insurances that offer protection to your staff? If not now, how can you plan to make security a reality in the future? Are there organizations you belong to, or could join, that would allow you the benefits of membership in a larger group? Are there fundraising efforts or benefactors in the community who might assist you in meeting these goals? Do you provide the proper tools, equipment, and materials needed to do the job? Do you set aside time to orient and train new staff? Do you provide quality in-service training and ongoing staff support? Are you a calm, stable, and dependable administrator — can staff count on your predictability and resourcefulness in responding to their needs?

Love/affiliation needs

Do members of your organization feel a sense of belonging? Do you give and receive support? Are there opportunities to develop satisfying relationships? Do you make opportunities to meet in small groups to discuss employee-management issues? Do you celebrate and/or acknowledge important milestones, holidays, birthdays, and special occasions? Do you express consideration of one another through notes, hospital visits, regular staff meetings, committees, employee newsletters, and bulletin boards? As an administrator, do you have an open-door policy?

Respect needs

Are staff given opportunities to display their special talents and skills? Do you have incentive plans or awards for achievement, attendance, and helpful suggestions? Do you promote and increase wages when you are able to do so? Do you provide plaques, certificates, and other recognition for service? Do you give individuals opportunities to explore new areas in their professional development? Do you share with the public your staff's accomplishments? As an administrator, do you give day-to-day recognition for a job well done?

Fulfillment needs

Does each job provide interesting mental and emotional challenge in a way that is valued by the person doing the job? Has each staff person identified goals for his or her personal and professional growth, and outlined steps to be taken on the job to meet those goals? Are there opportunities for freedom of expression and experimentation in the work? Do you encourage personal and professional growth and community involvement?

As an administrator, do you respect the values and self-fulfillment needs of your staff?

I believe that most of us work in child care because we hold very strong values about what is good and right for children in our world. Though our work can be overwhelming at times, we do have the power to change our thinking, to take important steps forward in improving our personal behavior and lifestyle, and to advocate for change in social policies that impact our industry. So what's stopping us?

Change is difficult

It requires effort and commitment. We get comfortable with the familiarity of our routines even if the ultimate consequences are negative. Sometimes we are just too tired to get started. We procrastinate. This week is just too hectic. The truth is, there is no week in the future that will be any less hectic than this week, but we delude ourselves into believing that the *right* time will show itself. Perhaps we put off doing all the things that would make us feel better, more capable and fulfilled because we bite off too big a piece and choose too narrow a time frame in which to achieve our goals.

How many times have we thought we would like to lose 20 pounds or stop smoking those 20 cigarettes a day? Of course, we want to shed those pounds or cigarettes immediately with the least amount of effort. We look at the entire 20 and realize it might take a year to be successful. A year seems hopeless. And so, we never begin. But, what if we focused on reducing by one pound or one cigarette a week? Somehow one pound or one cigarette does not seem enough, and yet, in a short time, we would be down by 20. Can we each make a commitment to begin with one small step? Can we help each other to stay the course?

Children have no voice if those who love them and care for them are too burned out and disillusioned to speak. To paraphrase Gandhi, "We must become the change we seek." Our work allows us to take these children, "so fresh from God," to enjoy them and to help shape them. Our work allows us to live our important values and beliefs each and every day, contributing something to the future of our world. We cannot continue to settle for less for either ourselves or our children. This calls for nothing short of a revolution in our personal lifestyles as well as our social attitudes and policies. Children matter, and so do those who care for them. It is no small thing to be loved by a child. It is no small thing to care for them with our love, our devotion, and our time. In our work with children, we are the instruments. We must keep our tools sharp and healthy.

Lilli-ann Buffin, MSW, is the owner of New Developments Family Enrichment Services in Wooster, Ohio. She develops programs for and about children and families. Lilli has worked as a child and family therapist, child care director, and educator.

Using Beginnings Workshop to Train Teachers by Kay Albrecht

Buffin gets right to the heart of the matter — teaching can be stressful, demanding, and anxiety producing as well as rewarding and meaningful. She considers the infrastructure that underpins our profession as lacking — a point of view that has a great deal of validity. What can teachers do? What can directors do?

The application of Maslow's framework of needs to the teaching profession offers some ideas. Pick a small group of teachers to meet with you to discuss this article. With a spoken spirit of trust, look at each level of need and identify what kinds of support are available for teachers at each level of need. See if you can operationalize some of the strengths and gaps you identified so that solutions can be generated. For example, as you discuss respect needs, identify specifically what you do to respect needs, like providing anniversary gifts based on tenure, and what you don't do but teachers feel they would like, like creating a peer teaching award and announcing it to parents and the community. This is strategic evaluation and planning at its best — and probably, at its hardest. Give it a shot — you will probably find you do a lot more than you thought, and you will certainly find new ideas that might work in your school.

Mentoring

MENTORING

Mentoring Teachers . . .
A Partnership in Learning

by Patricia Scallan-Berl

Training advice is easy to find these days. Books, videos, workshops, and seminars are everywhere. But ask a university professor, CEO, or master teacher how they acquired the knowledge and skills to successfully perform their jobs and they will rarely say they were guided by traditional methods of instruction. Rather, today's leaders, whether in the boardroom or the classroom, point to inspiring mentors, who were pivotal influences in helping them recognize and develop their own capabilities to excel (*Wall Street Journal*, 2002).

Within classroom settings, mentors can be the key to unlocking and developing teachers' talents. For many educators of young children, the very essence of teaching is a process of continual inquiry, discovery, and renewal. Yet, most teachers rarely have time in their daily teaching to reflect upon what happens in their classrooms, document their work, or study their own teaching practices. Through regular observations and discussions with a skilled mentor, teachers can begin to refine teaching practices, acquire new competencies, gain insight, and become more confident and effective educators.

Mentors can counter the pull of comfortable and ingrained classroom routines by helping teachers analyze and examine the tacit understandings that have developed around familiar practices (Terell, Klein, Jewett, 1998). With a mentor as a guide, a teacher, whose usual methods may not be working in a particular situation, can step back, reframe, change, or take a more experimental approach in her teaching. Through discussions, observations, and self-reflection, mentors encourage teachers to make new sense out of familiar situations and uncertainties and respond successfully to challenges.

What is a mentor?

The term mentor originates from the Greek mythological hero, Odysseus, who, prior to setting out for an extended journey to Troy, entrusts the education of his son, Temelecus, to his loyal friend Mentor. Odysseus instructs Mentor to tell the son all he knows. Modern usage defines mentoring as "to coach, tutor, train, give hints, or prime with fact." Training applications in industry and education use the term mentoring interchangeably with coaching. But regardless of the term used, the fundamental concept is the pairing of reflection and apprenticeship, when an older or more experienced individual passes down knowledge of how a task is done to someone who is less experienced.

A learning partnership over time

The focus of mentoring is on the acquisition of knowledge, core competencies, and career development. Framed within the context of an extended relationship over a longer period of time, mentors create a learning partnership between themselves and the individual, fostering feelings of competency, recognition, learning, accomplishment, and high performance. Through a series of supportive interactions teachers acquire knowledge, perspective, and self-awareness from their direct engagement with a mentor. Mentors, in turn, stimulate the teacher's own introspection, primarily through questions that facilitate insight or change in a teacher's behavior or perception, leading the way to greater skill, awareness, and defined outcomes. Timothy Gallwey, Harvard educator and tennis expert, describes mentoring, "as a way of unlocking a person's potential to maximize their own performance. It is helping them to learn rather than teaching them" (Whitmore, 2002).

Let the learning begin...

Gloria Steinem, noted feminist author, asserts, "The first problem for all of us men and women is not to learn, but to unlearn." Mentor relationships are effective because they help us to do just that. They challenge our thinking, causing us to critically reflect upon our current practices, moving us to action and transformation.

Mentoring works because it evolves from core principles of adult learning theory (Bell, 1998).

First, adults are motivated to learn as they develop needs and interests that learning will satisfy. In mentoring, we begin with the teacher's needs and interests as the appropriate starting points for setting goals.

Second, adult orientation to learning is usually life or work-centered. Mentor relationships begin with defining the focus of the relationship around life-and/or work related situations, not academic or theoretical subjects.

Third, experience is the richest resource for adult learning. Mentoring involves active participation in a planned series of experiences. Knowledge and competency are derived from the analysis of those experiences and their application to work and life situations.

Fourth, adults have a deep need to be self-directing. The characteristic style of mentors is to engage individuals in a process of inquiry, analysis, and decision-making, rather than to directly transmit knowledge and then evaluate the protege's conformity to it. Mentors encourage self-directed, independent, and collegial interactions over more hierarchical relationships.

Fifth, as individual differences among adult learners increase with age and experience, mentoring is well suited to make use of optimum provisions for differences in learning styles, pace of learning, content, culture, ethnicity, religion, gender, urgency, context, career life cycle, and aspirations.

Getting started

The process begins with the mentor inviting the teacher to identify "What do I want to learn, to change, to happen?" The mentor facilitates by helping the teacher explore the current situation and identify what the teacher is doing and what could ideally be done. This *reality check* is achieved through insights the teacher derives from discussions, observations, feedback, and self-reflection.

Next, the mentor and teacher explore the current situation and define a desired goal or outcome. The mentor asks, "What would be the most helpful thing for you to take away from this session?" Once a problem or goal is identified, the mentor encourages the teacher to consider options, alternative strategies, or new courses of action. Questions such as "What can you try?", "What happens if…?", or "What else could you do?"

frame the discussions and observations by the mentor. Once a goal is identified, the teacher implements the new plan, evaluates, modifies, and reflects back upon the results.

In facilitating goals or desired outcomes mentors should consider the following:

- An understanding of the principle issues.
- A vision or description of the desired outcome.
- A decision as to which way to proceed.
- A clear idea of the action steps.
- An agreed upon time frame for meeting the goal.
- An outline for the month that each can follow.
- A defined schedule for meeting.

Effective mentors are excellent observers who possess the ability to quickly assess and understand the teacher's skill level and needs. They are able to target their discussions and coaching to what is important to the teacher, developing rapport, and validation. While some mentors may be responsible for supervising others in the organization, it is best if the mentor is not a direct supervisor of the teacher, since supervisory relationships can easily introduce an evaluative quality to the feedback, hindering open communication and risk taking.

From feedback to insight

It has been said, "There is no wisdom like frankness." Leading management consultant and author, Ken Blanchard believes that honest feedback is critical to changing behavior. In the book, *Empowerment Takes More Than a Minute*, Blanchard writes that, "People without information cannot act responsibly. People with information are compelled to act responsibly." Without information, people cannot monitor themselves or make sound decisions. (Blanchard, Carlos, & Randolph, 1996). For Blanchard, sharing information through feedback is the first key to empowering people in organizations. It allows the individual to understand his or her current situation in clear terms. Sharing information through feedback builds trust throughout the organization and helps people to gain a greater sense of responsibility and ownership of their situations. Mentors encourage and facilitate the sharing of information by asking questions, probing, and helping to spark ideas that compel the teachers to search for answers and new perspectives.

Leading with questions

Effective mentors lead with questions, not answers. In the popular best seller *Good to Great*, author Jim Collins cites numerous examples of CEOs who create successful work climates by engaging their employees through questions. By opening up conversations with questions like, "What is on your mind?" or "What should we be concerned about?" leaders create a climate of open communication that allows the current business realities and struggles to bubble to the surface, be identified, discussed, and understood (Collins, 2001).

Like the CEOs in *Good to Great*, mentors, too, query teachers with open ended and probing questions that increase awareness and understanding. Here are some examples of questions mentors can use to help teachers reflect and gain insight (Whitmore, 2002):

- What is the hardest/most challenging part of this for you?
- What criteria are you using?
- What would be the consequences for you and others?
- What advice would you give to a friend in your situation?
- What would you gain/lose by doing/saying that?
- If someone said/did that to you, what would you feel/think/do?
- What would success in this challenge look like to you?
- What would be the first step you would need to take? Why?
- What should happen next?

In guiding teachers, mentors are careful to reflect back what they heard the teacher express and summarize points. This ensures correct understanding and reassurance that the learner is being fully heard and understood. Through discussion and analysis, mentors can validate the teacher's perspective as well as bring differing views to the discussion.

Choosing a mentor

A successful mentor program depends upon creating a climate of mutual trust, patient leadership, and emotional maturity. It requires a shared commitment of both time and goals. The following characteristics are important to keep in mind when choosing a mentor:

Balance — Because the mentoring partnership is grounded in mutuality, interdependence, and respect, emphasis is given early on to role clarity and expectations.

Respect — Partners recognize their differences while respecting their common needs and objectives. There is a spirit of generosity and acceptance rather than a focus on rules and rights.

Truthfulness — Mentors work hard to give feedback in a way that is caring, frank, and compassionately straightforward.

Trust and acceptance — There is a climate of experimentation, risk taking, and freedom to fail. Error is accepted as a necessary step on the path from novice to master.

Optimism — Mentors see teachers in terms of their future potential, not just past performance. They believe that people possess more capability than they are currently expressing (Whitmore, 2002).

Some Tips in Mentoring Gen X

James DeSena, consultant to Fortune 500 companies, offers these tips for mentoring Gen Xers. He suggests that when you mentor this age group, make the coaching more self-directed, self-paced, and self-evaluated. Begin the relationship by finding out what outcomes the individual would like to derive from the mentoring. Focus conversations on asking the right questions rather than trying to coach by offering the right answers. Work to make the training and discussion more interactive, taking advantage of a variety of training formats including face-to-face meetings, e-mail communication, online learning, and other professional development opportunities. Always communicate with the individual in ways that he or she prefers and finds most complementary to his or her learning style.

And remember that goals need to be directed not only at the skills and performance needed in the current situation but also at the skills that are needed and valued in the future. Reinforce and recognize the individual's progress and, most importantly, don't discount past experience. Rather, relate to it and build upon it.

Self-directed — Mentors follow the interests of the learner, monitoring how that relates to the problem or inquiry at hand. By refraining from asserting one's own interests, mentors gain the trust and confidence of the teacher since their interests and needs are respected.

Support — Good mentors don't rescue, they support. They resist the temptation to demonstrate a preferred way and instead steer the learning into a supportive direction through questions and observations. While mentors may on occasion demonstrate a technique, they continually ask themselves, will my demonstrations increase or decrease the learner's independence?

Acknowledgement — Mentors set aside time to reflect on the learner's success. They ask the teacher what made it successful, so that the individual can capitalize on it and experience a positive change process that is self-sustaining (Holliday, 2001).

Applications

As a practical form of professional development, mentoring lends itself to a myriad of applications including improving team communications, pinpointing the specific cause for an undesirable behavior, conducting classroom observations, addressing classroom management issues, implementing a new curriculum, conducting child assessments, resolving staff or parent conflicts, preparing for accreditation, or succession planning.

In responding to the ever present challenges of retaining quality staff and providing continual professional development, mentoring becomes an invaluable tool for developing the human assets within a center. Simply stated, mentoring is about fostering and developing a professional disposition toward lifelong learning.

Mentoring, when executed well, becomes a way of thinking, believing, and being. It is a process through which teachers can become reflective practitioners, capable of mentoring others. More than just a partnership based on good synergy, mentoring can become a catalyst for learning, high achievement, and personal fulfillment.

References

Bell, C. R. (1998). *Managers as Mentors*. Austin, TX: Bard Press.

Blanchard, K., Carlos, J., & Randolph, A. (1996). *Empowerment Takes More Than a Minute*. San Francisco: Berrett-Koehler Publishers.

Collins, J. (2001). *Good to Great*. New York: Harper Collins Publishers.

DeSena, J. (2002). Business Consultant and Speaker. Discussion. Jim DeSena, MBA, CSP, is a nationally recognized authority on leadership. He is the author of *Take the Lead and Win* (McGraw Hill, 2003), and president of Performance Achievement Systems, Inc. His web site, www.salesleaders.com, provides free articles, reports, and resources. He can be reached at 800-4321-WIN.

Holliday, M. (2001). *Coaching, Mentoring & Managing*. Franklin Lakes, NJ: The Career Press.

Hymowitz, C. (2002). "Effective Leaders Say One Pivotal Experience Sealed Their Careers." *Wall Street Journal*.

Tertell, E. A., Klein, S. M., & Jewett, J. L. (1998). *When Teachers Reflect*. Washington, DC: National Association for the Education of Young Children.

Whitmore, J. (2002). *Coaching for Performance*. London, UK: Nicholas Brealey Publishing.

Patricia Scallan-Berl is a division vice president of mid-Atlantic operations for Bright Horizons Family Solutions. She is known nationally as a conference presenter and author of articles in child care center management and supervision. She has been a regular contributor to *Exchange* since 1978. In addition to her lovely family, Patricia has a passion for orchids, Springer Spaniels, and travel.

Using Beginnings Workshop to Train Teachers by Kay Albrecht

Finding Your Own Mentors: Berl makes a strong case for using mentors for furthering your professional development. Do you have good mentors helping you learn and grow? If not, consider ways to find your own mentors — those more experienced who can help you grow professionally. Start by looking near you — at those people in your environment who might offer new skills, feedback, or opportunities for reflection about your abilities and growth areas. Then, look wider, outside your immediate environment for those who offer compatible or transferable skills.

Assessing Your Staff's Mentoring Potential: In order to form successful mentoring relationships, you must know who has the potential and the skills to mentor others. Take a critical look at your staff list with the goal of identifying those with the experience to serve as mentors for others. Select one or two of them to join you in becoming mentors to others.

Do I Fit the Bill?: Use the characteristics listed on page 65 as a self-assessment for those who choose to learn to mentor with you. After completing this step, discuss your self-evaluation with someone who can help you reflect on the accuracy of your self-view and maybe, in the process, become a mentor to you.

Mentor Versus Teacher Q-Sort: Berl differentiates between mentoring (reflective apprenticeship by a more experienced person) and teaching new skills or knowledge to others. This difference hints at an important component of mentoring — it must be voluntary and mutual to really succeed. To explore this voluntary component of mentoring and to find out who might be able to mentor whom on your staff as well as who could teach, explore mentoring with teachers using a Q-sort technique. Make this a personal, reflective experience, perhaps completing it during discussions of challenges or competency evaluations. Put each teacher's name on a 3" x 5" index card. Ask the teacher you are working with to put the cards into two piles — people they would like to learn new things from and those they would like to be mentored by. Once there are two piles, ask the teacher to put each pile in order — from their first choice of a mentor and teacher to their last. Finally, ask the teacher to identify what she would like to learn from the first person on the teacher list and what areas she would like mentoring in from the first person on the mentor list.

This process will give directors a good idea of who is interested in being taught and who is interested in being mentored — and the opportunity to help connect mentoring pairs who are inclined to work with each other. It will also give you a good idea who staff see in coaching and teaching roles as well.

Learning to Mentor: Form a small group of willing mentors and begin the process of learning how to mentor together. Start by reading the articles in this Beginnings Workshop, then move on to learning how to ask good questions, problem solving about frustrations or failed attempts, discussing observations, identifying when a teacher needs teaching vs. mentoring, and so forth. Meet regularly to share your successes and learn from each other. (Caution!: Discuss how you will honor the confidentiality of the teachers you are mentoring during these discussions. Make sure that the group avoids the pitfall of comparing the teachers you are mentoring.)

Where to Start?: Berl lists many applications for mentoring (see p. 65). Take her list as a starting place for new mentors, picking one application at a time for new mentors to explore. Taking mentoring in small, manageable segments will enhance feelings of competency for new mentors.

MENTORING

The Potential Gains of Peer Mentoring Among Children

by Leslie Moguil

The historical perspective of what is currently being identified as "peer mentoring" has been found to be a natural component of belonging to a large family, an extended family, a one-room schoolhouse, or a mixed aged classroom. Seizing the general tendency of children to help other children, which occurs almost spontaneously in this type of environment, can be successfully replicated within current learning institutions.

Young children acting as human resources for their peers in schools, after school programs, summer programs, community centers, and a variety of programs where children of different ages and abilities come together is beginning to take root. Adults in the form of teachers, counselors, administrators, librarians, and others have taken the initiative to create the structure and provide the support to students and adults in carrying out a variety of creative peer mentoring programs. The account that follows focuses on the development and implementation of a Buddy Reading program at the RCMA Wimauma Academy, a charter school located in rural Hillsborough County, Florida.

Three years ago the Redlands Christian Migrant Association embarked on a journey to develop and design the structure of its first two charter schools. The structure of one of those schools includes grades K-2 and grades 6-8. The target student population consists of a majority of students who are acquiring English as a non-native language. The challenge being addressed is how to take a group of students who have been previously identified as reading below grade level in middle school, and enable them to feel positive and successful about something they have been struggling with throughout their school careers — reading.

The split grade level structure, which is clearly out of the ordinary, was designed with the intent of utilizing the potential created by middle school children interacting with primary grade students in a partnership for learning. The goal of building self-esteem and strengthening the reading skills of both age groups through mentoring is now becoming a cornerstone of the curriculum.

The program takes shape in what RCMA Wimauma Academy students and staff members refer to as "Buddy Reading." Every Friday middle school students are paired with elementary students in the confines of their primary classrooms to read to each other, and on occasion, to read aloud simultaneously. Second graders rush to the classroom shelf to choose the books and are often observed giving their older buddies a voice in the decision of which book to tackle first. Every nook and cranny in the classroom becomes a place where the partners stretch out, get comfortable, and read.

Buddy Reading is a natural complement to the existing Accelerated Reading (AR) Program adopted by the school. The AR program is based on teachers and students working cooperatively in setting reading goals based on an assessment of where the children are within their individual reading continuum. The classroom and library contain books that reflect the different reading levels of the children. The program is supported by computer technology that allows children to test their comprehension upon completion of a book. The role of the teacher is to support the students in their understanding of the system in which books are labeled for their use; to provide structured time for children to read; to help students set appropriate reading goals; to motivate students to read; to track progress and celebrate the attainment of the students' AR goals.

When the middle school reading buddies arrive in the classroom they take on a much different demeanor than is present at other times of the school day. The characteristic teenage ego, along with the strong desire to demonstrate their ability to assert themselves, seems to disappear as they come face to face with their younger reading buddy. The younger buddies approach with a smile, eager and pleased to have the attention of an older student focused solely on them. How often do students have the opportunity to have one on one support during the school day? The obvious answer is very little, but students know they can count on Buddy Reading every Friday.

From the perspective of the middle school student it may be more difficult to identify what potential this mentoring partnership plays in their educational experience. The obvious gain, as is true for all positive mentoring experiences is the development of one's own self esteem, derived from the participation in an act of service. When older students engage in the act of making a difference, they are paving the way to improving their own social skills and developing positive values for the future.

The potential gains move well beyond the social skill boundary and into academic achievement for those students who have never read on grade level. The embarrassment of continually stumbling over words and the frustration of being told how important reading is, only to continue to fall farther and farther behind your peers, perpetuates the formation of a wall. This wall stands in the way of successful student achievement in the learning of subject area content. The more students read and the more they feel success in their ability to read, the greater their potential to succeed in a broad range of critical content areas.

Buddy Reading provides for an environment that is positive and non-threatening for all students involved, especially those students who are reading below grade level. The program also provides a challenge for those readers who are on or above grade level by enabling them to utilize and highlight their reading strengths.

The concept of Buddy Reading has moved beyond the classroom and into the homes of the students. Students are encouraged to participate in Buddy Reading at home. During a recent circle time, a group of second grade students shared who their home reading buddies were. Older brothers, sisters, and cousins were mentioned as people whom children do read with. Beyond this level of experience, several second grade children mentioned that they read to younger siblings or cousins on a regular basis. These young children are now on the path to becoming informal mentors to yet another group of even younger children. This continues to perpetuate the feeling of success coupled with the enjoyment of reading.

In order to strengthen the Buddy Reading program and the partnership for learning that has been developed with the students, Augustin Montejo, charter school coordinator, has asked the middle and primary school students for their feedback on the reading program currently in place. Several students expressed their desire to have a consistent reading buddy in order to strengthen their knowledge about the child they are working with and increase their ability to improve the child's reading skills. Plans are in order to conduct an interest survey with students regarding their book preferences prior to the purchase of new library books. Additional efforts to involve parents and community volunteers are also under way.

Empowering children with a voice and making them part of the mission to help others within their own school community has proven to be invaluable for the staff, children, and families of the RCMA Wimauma Academy.

Leslie Moguil accepted a position with Redlands Christian Migrant Association in 1987 as an education coordinator for multiple child care centers. She was responsible for the delivery of a quality educational program for migrant and rural poor children birth to five years of age and has mentored numerous RCMA employees toward setting and achieving their professional development goals. In her most recent position as special projects coordinator, Leslie provides administrative and development support to over 70 RCMA programs located in 20 rural Florida counties. She has facilitated training at local, state, and national conferences on education, and issues related to farm worker advocacy. She serves as a member of the Florida Department of Education's Migrant Education Advisory Council, CDA Advisor, editor of the RCMA HOY monthly newsletter, and is a federal reviewer for Head Start.

Using Beginnings Workshop to Train Teachers by Kay Albrecht

Buddy Reading for Me!: Implement a buddy reading program in your center. Consider good matches between age groups (like enough differences between ages to have buddies view the opportunity as a special treat) as well as between individual children.

Creating Many Mentoring Opportunities: Explore other ways children might mentor. Consider cross age mentors, like kindergarteners introducing new toys and materials to twos, as well as same age mentors, like competent climbers teaching climbing skills to new climbers. Don't forget to consider developmental stages as well like non-napping children helping younger children calm down and go to sleep or skilled snack self-servers staffing the self-serve snack area for new self-servers.

MENTORING

Mentoring Advocates in the Context of Early Childhood Education

by Sessy I. Nyman

Advocates have been a critical component in every social movement that effects change. Whether we examine the Civil Rights movement, the Women's Movement, or the movement to create a public K-12 educational system, movements are made up of individual advocates. Types of advocates and how they create change vary greatly, but what ties them together is their common goal.

In the field of early childhood education, we have the foundation for an effective, broad-based coalition of advocates; there is much work to be done. Growing our advocacy community must be a high priority for everyone who cares for the future of young children — one advocate at a time. The work of each and every advocate is critical if we are to reach our goal of high quality early learning and education for each child.

Advocates are people who bring an issue to life

There are no specific prerequisites for being an advocate. Most people advocate for something every day of their lives. It is in our nature when we believe in something or have a passion for the issue. The challenge lies in being an effective advocate — connecting the day to day work to a larger movement.

The Day Care Action Council of Illinois (DCACI) is a statewide advocacy organization, one of the few in the state to have a full time lobbyist who works with elected officials to further an agenda that supports high quality care and education for all young children. DCACI has a broad membership base of child care providers, parents, and other advocates. The strength of the agency does not lie only in its legislative relationships and policy know-how but equally on its grassroots constituency.

In the spring of 2002, the Illinois Child Care Assistance Program faced drastic cuts that would have crippled child care providers and devastated low-income families already struggling to keep their children in high quality programs. Over the course of 10 weeks, thousands of parents and child care providers across the state wrote letters, called their legislators, and rallied at the Capitol. In the end, no cuts were levied against the program — one of very few social service support programs that were not cut in a year of severe budget shortfall.

The key was not the access DCACI had to policy makers, nor was it the relationship DCACI had with community providers and parents statewide. Instead, it was the combination of both that made its advocacy efforts so effective. Individual advocate's actions were multiplied and made more effective because they were part of a larger campaign.

It is most effective when advocates come from a wide array of fields and interests to create a broad foundation for support. With a diverse foundation, an issue is brought to life for a variety of constituencies, in a variety of ways that more people can relate to and understand. Our challenge, as early childhood advocates, is to make the issue of high quality care and education for young children everyone's issue. If it remains only *our* issue, we will never be successful.

In Illinois we have long worked to engage the business community as advocates for early care and education. Because they have a different constituency than either the *typical* parent or provider advocate, they speak from a business, workforce, or economic perspective of why child care matters. They often have networks and friends that early care and education advocates may not be able to access. Clearly, growing our advocacy community in numbers and diversity is critical to broad-based support and long-term change.

Our goal is to make everyone an early childhood advocate: professional advocacy groups, researchers, elected officials, child care providers, pre-school and K-3 teachers, parents, community members, members of the business community, civic organizations, and unions. Many voices singing the same chorus is always more effective in creating change.

The role of mentors

Everyone has the capacity to be an advocate, but to be an effective advocate takes time and support. This is the role of the mentor in building advocates. Mentors can be many things to many people; the key is to be the right thing at the right time.

Any mentor, no matter what the issue or circumstance, needs to recognize the individual capacities of the person they mentor. One of the biggest mistakes a mentor can make is to measure one person against another, or worse, against him/herself. Just as there are advocates from all walks of life, there are individuals with different levels of ability and commitment.

In its simplest form, the role of a mentor is to recognize each advocate's abilities and then build upon them. Understanding the starting point of a potential advocate will define the long process of mentoring the individual's potential.

Consider this scenario: Sylvia was a life-long advocate now in a position to bring others along. She had been a central decision-maker to the children's movement, marched on Washington too many times to remember, established personal relationships with her local and national legislators, and effected change for children for over 20 years. She is a born advocate and wants to nurture future advocates and leaders for children. To her peers and fellow life-long advocates, Sylvia is a natural leader and thus, a natural mentor.

She is excited to share what she knows with others, so they too might become effective advocates for children. However, early on she became frustrated when a mentee did not participate in Saturday meetings, was unable to commit to national trainings, and did not feel comfortable speaking to large audiences. After a short time Sylvia told her mentee that he did not have the qualities to be an effective advocate. She put the fault on the mentee, but the fault was in her skills as a mentor. A huge opportunity was lost.

From the beginning, Sylvia defined the criteria by her personal standards and skills; she did not begin with a clear understanding of the starting point for her mentee's emerging leadership. Instead of building a life-long advocate, she convinced a potential advocate that *he didn't have what it takes*.

To be an effective mentor, it is important to remember that the charge is not to clone yourself, but instead to identify skills and potential in the person you are mentoring and then to nurture the development of those skills. Sylvia could have nurtured the personal relationships the mentee already possessed, set up one-one-one meetings rather than creating large group settings, and built on the personal experience and knowledge of the mentee to help him begin to see his advocacy potential. In time, the confidence of the new advocate grows, and he or she looks for new challenges and opportunities for growth.

Ultimately, a mentor is charged with developing skills in a potential advocate, as well as:

■ helping *'beginner advocates'* recognize that they are already advocates, and what they already do, however small, makes a difference.

■ helping grow and nurture advocacy efforts — looking not only at skill but context and reach.

■ demonstrating to the advocate how his or her efforts fit into a larger movement.

■ helping the advocate identify key relationships they currently have, and encouraging them to establish new relationships that will extend the reach and impact of their work.

■ supporting the advocate in the pieces of advocacy that are new, until the advocate feels comfortable doing it on his or her own.

■ encouraging every advocate to be a leader and continually reaching out to engage new advocates committed to the same goals.

Part of a movement

In reality we are all part of a state, national, and even international movement that supports high quality care and education for all children. This is a big concept for many advocates to get their arms around. It is always important to be aware of the larger movement or vision, while at the same time making the issue local and real. When an issue has immediate impact on local children, it is much easier to build a broad base of support.

All advocates must be part of a movement, group, or network that can directly affect public policy. Policy is the primary way to create overarching, long-lasting change. While the work that happens in our neighborhood, our school district, or our town are all important, unless they connect to the larger public policy process, real change will not occur.

What an advocate needs

Passion is the essence, the necessary requirement for advocacy. It provides the essential foundation upon which other advocacy skills can be built. A review of the following list can help gauge an advocate's skill and knowledge level, whether the advocate is you or someone you are mentoring. Knowing where you are at the beginning points you in the direction of where you need to grow — this is an important first step in mentoring an advocate.

■ **Understanding the issue.** Many advocates understand the issue from their own perspective or experiences. However, in order to build support and ownership of the issue among others, understanding the entire issue, with all its complexities, is critical. It is essential to be able to explain the issue and its importance to people who might not be early childhood professionals or who do not have young children.

■ **The context.** Knowing at least part of the history of an issue is critical to mapping out where it will go. Why has ECE emerged today as such an important issue? What has changed to increase demand? How have our expectations changed for young children? What is the role of ECE?

■ **Messaging.** The work of creating a message or building support happens in two primary categories:

1. Creating public will is central to the work of an advocate. If the general public does not support a concept or an issue, then the chances that change will happen are slim. Having a broad range of support and demonstrating need and effect is important in building public will.

2. Creating political commitment largely depends on the ability to create public will and to make sure elected officials know that the public supports the issue. We do this in a variety of ways, including relationship building, networking, public education, and media exposure. Just as it is important that advocates individually work towards a common goal, so too is it critical that the work comes together in a common message.

■ **Relationship building.** Relationships are built over time, by establishing trust, respect, and common interests. Whether engaging an elected official, other advocates, parents, or community members, relationships are crucial to an advocate's success. Understanding that a relationship goes beyond the current issue or campaign is critical for a new advocate.

■ **Understanding the players.** Who are the players? They are anyone and everyone you interact with, who cares about your issue, who is effected by your advocacy work, or even who might take a contrary view of your issue. They are also the leaders on your issue — the people making decisions, the people people listen to, and the people who have made a difference in the past. While everyone is important in turning

Ten Commandments of Policy Advocacy

Start with a base. Your base should reflect the breadth and diversity of support for your issue.

Work on a bi-partisan basis. This is the only way to avoid gridlock between the two chambers and the executive.

Cultivate a legislative champion in each house. Advocates, grassroots supporters, and lobbyists can only do so much; the sponsor must be a committed advocate when the legislation is debated.

Create a simple message that explains your issue, and then make sure that your supporters repeat it, over and over again.

Develop human-interest stories to demonstrate your points. Do not underestimate the power of anecdotes.

Organize a creative coalition in support of the issue. The most effective coalition partners lend an element of surprise; they are not expected to support the issue and may have opposed you before.

Activate your grassroots support. Legislators care most about issues that affect their own constituents. At the state or local level (not Congress), their unique letters or telephone calls create an impression of widespread support or opposition on all but the most controversial issues — on the same theory that ten cockroaches in a kitchen appear to be an infestation.

Be ready to compromise. No policy of government ever looks the same as when it was proposed.

Never lie or mislead a policy-maker about the importance of an issue, the opposition's position or strength, or any other matter. Your word is your bond.

Use the media to focus on public debate and to generate interest in the issue. Legislators and policy-makers are especially sensitive to media approval and criticism.

Prepared by Julie E. Hamos and Associates, September 1998

an issue into policy, the players are the faces that the general public connects with the issue.

■ **Why should anyone else care?** Early childhood care and education affects every segment of our society. An effective advocate will be able to explain how the issue affects different populations in different ways. The reasons why a parent cares about early childhood care may be different from why the local Chamber of Commerce cares. Both are important. The cost-benefit model of investing in quality early care and education is just as compelling to some legislators as the new research on brain development in infants is to others. By working with advocates from various fields, you learn how to craft your message in order to reach a variety of populations which helps you to ultimately be successful.

Thinking of advocacy skills in these ways will enable a mentor to help advocates recognize their skills and potential, and then to nurture strengths, overcome weaknesses, and understand the context.

Mentoring change

Change happens in a variety of ways, and a good mentor can ensure that each venue and opportunity for advocacy is the most effective it can be. As a young person entering the world of community activism and advocacy, I needed the leadership, guidance, and inspiration of mentors so that I could see my potential and the possibilities for change.

It is appropriate to write this article now, as the climate in our nation is not one conducive to highlighting the deficiencies in our various systems. States are facing major budget shortfalls, and critical services like child care and other early learning opportunities are being cut; some to the point of their collapse.

This is also a time of great opportunity for change. There is a national awakening around the importance of early brain development and the critical impact of high quality early learning opportunities for children from birth to five. There is growing concern in the business and education communities that if we don't invest in our very youngest learners, then we can never expect to have successful students and productive professionals in the future.

Now is the time to become an advocate, mentor an advocate, and grow our community of advocates for high quality early learning for all children.

Sessy Nyman is the Vice President of Public Policy and Government Relations of Illinois Action for Children. Before becoming Vice President in 2001, Sessy started her career at with the agency in 1999 as the Community Organizer and Lobbyist for the Program. Sessy has her B.A. in Government and International Relations from The University of South Carolina and her M.S. in Cultural Geography from The University of Massachusetts-Amherst. She has presented both locally and nationally on early childhood policy issues. Sessy divides her time between the legislature in Springfield, visiting parents and providers around the state, and her office in Chicago. Sessy is married and has one daughter.

MENTORING

Is Mentoring Parents A Piece of Cake?

by Miriam Mercado Mercado

1 C respect
1 C consistency
2 C encouragement
1 C communication
1 C coffee with cream and lots of sugar

Sprinkle with strength.
Stir with care.
Bake in a warm friendly environment.
Cook until confidence develops.
Serve with opportunities.

An active and healthy community is one that has the collaboration and partnership of its residents, stakeholders, and families to create an environment that is healthy, safe, and full of opportunities and hope for children's growth, development, and success.

El Centro believes in providing opportunities for parents to be leaders in the community and advocates for their children. El Centro de Desarrollo y Reafirmación Familiar illustrates a clear commitment to the concepts of familia, identidad, y comunidad (family, identity, and community).

For families and staff associated with El Centro the relationship of the caregiver and child is central to parenting. Simultaneously, parenting is seen as taking place in the context of the family's relationships with others, including family members, friends, and neighborhood institutions such as the workplace, schools, community individuals, and community-based organizations.

Parents and staff believe economic, political, and social forces influence families and individuals, thus recognizing the need

for families to have training in the skills of parenting but we also work to create opportunities that will lead parents to changes in attitude and behavior and help them develop the skills to advocate for concepts of familia, identidad, y communidad.

In order to accomplish these goals, families need access to educational resources, and employment opportunities, and they need the chance to be active members within the neighborhood. My position as a director of the family center offers me the opportunity to be a good mentor who can provide guidance, support, and create consciousness about the concepts of familia, identidad, y comunidad.

My focus is on the positive side. I am deeply aware that my role is not the role of a typical child care director. I am a coach, facilitator, educator, nurturer, trainer, and confidant for families as well as staff (who may also be parents). As a mentor I offer a supportive environment that helps parents at the center to build a relationship founded on trust and confidence. We see that this trust helps motivate the family and individuals to participate actively in their own growth and that of their children.

The atmosphere of the center is one of acceptance and invites parents to come: they feel like they are at home. Once they are at the center there are other parents who share similar concerns and hopes that are listened to by each other and the providers. Through this interaction and reflective process, parents have an opportunity to see that the providers at the center also care for the well-being of their families and community. The link happens immediately. Families get involved in carrying on the center's mission.

A supportive environment helps to establish a good relationship with parents by making families feel welcome and respected but not intruded upon. Communication is crucial. As providers we need to listen to family concerns. By showing trust and respect more than anything else we make them feel that they have the capacity to control their lives.

A couple of years ago a mother of three children was referred to the services at the family center. I remember when she came to the center for the first time. She had the need to talk, and she talked for hours. I was very impressed with her knowledge, vocabulary, love, and commitment for her children and her determination to provide her children a healthy and safe environment.

At that particular moment I saw a mother equipped with many skills, but she was so isolated that she could not recognize how fortunate she was. I offered her the opportunity to participate in a parenting group that provided activities for parent and child interaction, and I offered her a couple of hours to do volunteer work at the center. She blossomed like a flower in spring that is cultivated and nurtured with care and love. She became the president of the parent board. She enhanced her skills to a level that today she is making a difference in the community; she is running for a position on the Hartford Board of Education.

When families come to the center and are isolated, when they have no family, no resources, they seek a sense of family — someone to listen to them, to make connections, and to have the opportunities to break down the isolation they feel.

The center becomes an important space were the concept of familia is enhanced. It is important to look at the strength families bring with them and make them feel welcomed by creating an atmosphere that is comfortable — where they can participate and contribute in their own ways. The family center has a particular way to celebrate events that embraces families' participation during the planning and implementation. The center produces an annual Children's Festival with the participation of parents, residents, and other organizations in the neighborhood. The parent board plans the whole event by writing letters, asking for donations, finding activities and materials for the children, getting the guest speakers — everything. Parents take the lead in the festival and encourage other parents to take an active part in it.

Once you establish an environment that influences the comfort of parents that come to the center on a regular basis, you have the opportunity to build the relationship and develop a sense of confidence. This part of development is crucial because this is the time to offer the opportunity to parents to contribute to the well being of the community. Parents will enhance and strengthen the skills they already have if we allow them to grow, and they will transfer these skills to grow their children.

The mentoring relationship at this level is to model the exchanges between the mentor and parent so that the parent can use these models with their children. At the same time the parent can take those skills to be used for their own benefit and use them in their own community. It is important to offer parents a role where they feel valued and where their contribution is shared in an environment of camaraderie and solidarity.

It is essential that parents have the opportunity to develop confidence by participating actively in the organization's programming. Our agency has a board of directors that is run by the parents who are participating in our programs. The board of directors is a governing body that has a strong voice that advocates to meet the needs of the families that participate in our program and community.

Parents have always been involved in key decisions of the family center. Parent involvement and decision–making is high. While seeking funding for the family center, parents were involved in a community engagement process. In order to accomplish this task parents were trained, went into the community, and conducted the survey. The information gathered in this survey is being used to continue programs and activities and determine new ones.

There is no doubt that by giving families meaningful experiences with achievable outcomes, parents become empowered to make good decisions for their children and community. They feel supported, connected, and confident. They truly became leaders.

Los padres siempre han estado involucrados en las decisiones claves e importante del Centro de Familia. La toma de decisiones por parte de los padres es de mucho compromiso y respeto. Mientras se buscaba fondos para el Centro de Familia, los padres estaban involucrados en un proyecto de investigación e interacción con la comunidad Para poder alcanzar esta meta los padres fueron adiestrados, luego fueron a la comunidad y llevaron acabo la encuesta. La información que se logro recopilar en esta encuesta nos ha servido para continuar los programas del Centro de Familia y desarrollar otros nuevos.

No hay duda de que al darle a los padres oportunidades a tener experiencias significativas podemos alcanzar grandes y positivos resultados. Los padres alcanzan un alto nivel de autodeterminación al hacer decisiones para sus hijos y comunidad. Los padres se sienten apoyados, conectados y en confianza. Ellos verdaderamente se convierten en lideres.

Miriam Mercado is a program director at the Institute for the Hispanic Family/Catholic Family Services. She is responsible for the daily operations and the fiscal oversight management of Centro de Desarrollo y Reafirmación Familiar and Paraiso Infantil Day Care. Her background and experience has been around early childhood education and family advocacy issues. Miriam is a founder of Paders Abriendo Puertas, an advocacy Hispanic organization that works with parents who have children with disabilities as well as a strong advocate for children and women rights. As a volunteer she is involved in several organizations that advocate for children's and families' well being. She has a Masters Degree in Education from Cambridge College, Massachusetts.

Using Beginnings Workshop to Train Teachers by Kay Albrecht

Role Change?: Mercado suggests that directors embrace the role of mentoring parents as a viable alternative to teaching parenting skills. How viable an idea is this in your program? To explore the application, try it with one or two parents, approaching the relationship from this special point of view. Start conversations for these interactions with Mercado's question, "How can I help?"

Parents as Mentors for Each Other: Consider applying Mercado's ideas to a parent-mentoring program. Recruit parents to start small by contacting newly enrolled families to welcome them to the school and see what happens next. You may need to support this effort with mentor meetings to share strategies and successes.

MENTORING

Developing Effective Advocates: The Key to Effecting Lasting Change for Children

by Jonah Edelman

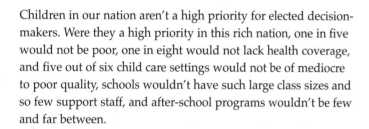

Children in our nation aren't a high priority for elected decision-makers. Were they a high priority in this rich nation, one in five would not be poor, one in eight would not lack health coverage, and five out of six child care settings would not be of mediocre to poor quality, schools wouldn't have such large class sizes and so few support staff, and after-school programs wouldn't be few and far between.

The core reason why decisionmakers don't prioritize children is that children and adults who care deeply about children's well-being lack the fundamental element that wins public resources: political power. Children don't vote or give political contributions, and, while we have numbers on our side, those of us who stand for children aren't organized into a powerful lobby.

Stand for Children is building that advocacy voice for children one community at a time. Since 1999, we've developed a uniquely effective grassroots child advocacy approach and an accompanying array of training and support that enables us to develop citizens from a wide range of backgrounds into highly effective advocates. Those advocates build local chapters — local citizen lobby groups — capable of effecting multiple changes for children over time. Following is a summary of Stand for Children's advocacy approach from the perspective of a citizen advocate, with a corresponding description of the support and training we provide.

Stand for children's advocacy approach

Get Started. We first work with local advocates to figure out their geographic focus area (generally one city or county) and to learn how to speak effectively about Stand for Children. Next, because collective leadership at every stage is essential, we work with them to recruit at least four other members who want to

organize the chapter. The initial five or more members make up a core group.

Come to Stand for Children's Leadership Conference. At least three members from a community (again, the focus on collective leadership development) come to a weekend training to learn key chapter-building skills and tools. With a heavy emphasis on role playing, we teach the leadership conference participants:

- How to build chapter teams through face-to-face conversations, introductory meetings, presentations, and then how to manage those teams on an ongoing basis.
- How to run effective meetings.
- How to facilitate in such a way as to discern the most broadly, deeply felt concerns in a group (as opposed to the normal pattern of eliciting a long list of concerns, which leaves participants with no idea of where to focus).
- How to do community fact-finding in order to learn how and when local decisions are made that affect children.
- How to assess a decisionmaker's position on a chapter issue, and
- How to run a community meeting during which the chapter directly asks local decisionmakers for their support.

Host a Half-Day Local Chapter-Building Workshop. The purpose of this workshop is twofold. It is a way to teach additional members the fundamentals of Stand for Children's advocacy approach and equip them to move forward in building chapter teams at their child care centers, congregations, schools, workplaces, etc. In addition, workshops teach the chapter leaders who attended the leadership conference how to teach. To facilitate this critical area of development staff send user-friendly session overviews to the chapter leaders ahead of time and then hold an in-depth practice session the day before the workshop.

Build at least three teams. Stand for Children chapters are made up of chapter teams (structured groups of five to 50 members formed within existing institutions or based on already existing relationships). Teams create multiple leadership roles with basic, doable responsibilities and, in the half-day workshop, we have developed structured training and ongoing support systems to help leaders learn those roles.

Teams must have at least two coordinators in order to create sustainability and shared leadership. Each team recruits members, hears concerns from its members, generates possible solutions, and researches those solutions. Teams generate turnout for chapter actions. The three team requirement ensures that a chapter has a broad enough base to take effective action.

Form a strategy team made up of representatives from each chapter team. The strategy team — the chapter steering committee — decides which of the team issues to pursue further. After chapter members meet with decisionmakers and other community members to figure out what solution is most achievable, the strategy team chooses the chapter's first "ask," and figures out an action strategy.

Take action on the first chapter issue. It may take a while to win, but persistence pays off. While sometimes a win comes quickly, in other cases it can take months, even years. Once a chapter wins on its first issue, chapter leaders and members feel an incredible sense of power and confidence. This is a key turning point in the development of effective advocates.

Elect chapter officers. Standard officer positions are chair, membership coordinator, and secretary-treasurer. Some chapters elect additional officers based on their needs.

Move the chapter forward. After electing officers and taking action, the chapter is founded. The goal is to keep getting stronger, keep pushing on the first issue if necessary, and then move toward taking on more and bigger issues. Once a chapter is founded, the development of advocates is by no means done.

Ongoing work with chapter leaders

Leaders in Stand for Children take on a significant level of responsibility. In small and mid-sized communities, they are expected to organize and sustain their chapters with staff consultation and support, as opposed to leaders relying on staff to organize the chapter for them.

Stand for Children foster the continued development of chapter leaders in a variety of ways:

■ *Regular coaching sessions.* From the beginning, staff organizers have regular face-to-face meetings or (if the chapter is at a distance from the staff person) calls with chapter-in-formation leaders. Some keys to making the coach-leader relationship effective include: initial and ongoing relationship-building to create trust and the space for constructive feedback, a healthy complement of affirmation in every coaching session, detailed reports by the chapter leaders in order to inform the agenda for the sessions, and continued use of role plays to help chapter leaders hone key skills.

■ *Half-day workshops.* Eventually, chapter leaders lead their own half-day chapter building workshops.

■ *Organizing with chapter leaders.* In addition to the workshops and regular coaching sessions, organizers develop the leadership of chapter leaders by "running with" them in order to model for them and give them first-hand feedback.

■ *201 level leadership conferences.* Stand for Children offers an intermediate level leadership conference track for experienced leaders, which covers more advanced topics such as using the electoral process effectively, media, and effective meeting facilitation. In addition, we encourage experienced chapter leaders to teach introductory leadership conference sessions.

■ *Peer mentorship and idea exchange.* Chapter leaders also develop through the support and mentorship of peers throughout the country. Stand for Children has created a listserv to enable leaders to share ideas and successes.

Stand for Children's advocacy approach and accompanying training and support have yielded solid results on two levels. First of all, we're impacting children's lives. In the past four years, Stand for Children chapters have won 32 local and state successes that have helped more than 180,000 children and secured more than $45 million for children's programs and services. Equally as important, we're developing effective advocates for the long run. The story of Stand for Children's first chapter in Salem, Oregon, which I organized and have supported for the past three years, exemplifies this combination of outcomes.

A case study: Salem, Oregon

After moving to Oregon from Washington, DC in late 1998 to test Stand for Children's fledgling advocacy model, I decided to organize Stand for Children's first chapter in the politically strategic but conservative state capital of Salem, as opposed to the more obvious choice of Portland. I started off in January 1999 by calling through a list of congregations that had hosted a Children's Sabbath celebration in prior years. From those cold calls, I got several rejections and one meeting. That meeting led to others. Eventually, I began to recruit some members with leadership potential, mostly from local congregations.

By late spring, the chapter had grown to more than 100 members, and its leaders — who ranged from a community college professor of early childhood education to a Head Start family service worker to the head of the local chapter of Habitat for Humanity to the pastor of the local Congregational Church to a part-time children's therapist who considered herself "just a concerned mom" — decided to use their strength to try to reverse their county's egregious decision to cut five children's mental health therapists.

In my first few months, through face-to-face conversations, I began to recruit some members with leadership potential, mostly from local congregations. The turning point, however, was meeting Randy Fishfader, a community college professor of early childhood education and member of Temple Beth Sholom who has become Stand for Children's standard-bearing leader. By late spring, the chapter had grown to more than 100 members, and leaders decided to use their strength to try to reverse their county's egregious decision to cut five children's mental health therapists. In the course of just one month, with my support, chapter leaders researched possible sources of funds to reinstate the funds — including eliminating a high-priced new administrator and using reserves — held meetings with all three county commissioners and the acting county manager (who had made the decision). Despite being ignored and even criticized in these initial meetings, the chapter moved forward in organizing an accountability session with the county commissioners. Three hundred eighty people attended. The shocked county commissioners agreed to look into the funding sources chapter leaders suggested and agreed to empower a task force that eventually ended up achieving significant changes in the county's managed care mental health system. Two days later, at a final morning budget hearing attended by 100 chapter members, the commissioners reinstated three of the five counselors.

After that initial breakthrough, which generated a tremendous sense of power on the part of every leader who was involved as well as a significant amount of expertise, I scaled back to half-time support. The chapter moved on to address the acute dental health needs of low-income children in Salem by recruiting "neighborhood dentists" who are assigned to treat children in pain at 39 local elementary schools, winning county and city funding for a dental disease prevention educator who teaches professionals to teach new and expectant parents to prevent decay and infection, and pursuing funding for a comprehensive school-based dental health education program modeled on a program at the low-income school where the dental issues first came to light.

Having instilled Stand for Children's culture and core practices — including starting and ending meetings on time, having clear goals, written agendas, and prepared roles for every meeting, incorporating next steps and evaluation into every activity, focusing on relationship building — and having developed a solid, diverse leadership group — which numbered four core leaders (including the chapter's outstanding chair Randy Fishfader) and more than 20 secondary leaders — I then pulled back further.

At this point, I spend just one to two hours per week on average coaching Randy Fishfader and a few other Salem chapter leaders, who are now rightly recognized for their leadership by decisionmakers and community members alike. As is the goal of our advocacy model, the Salem chapter, whose development has challenged and inspired chapter leaders across Oregon and the country, continues to grow its membership (it now has 650 members), organize new chapter teams (there are 15), and take on bigger community initiatives.

Something of a defining moment came just a few months ago at a lunch meeting between the mayor, city council president, Randy Fishfader, Christine Ertl (the mother of two young children who insisted the first time we met that she "was just a mom" and had nothing to add to an organization like Stand for Children), and Merrily McCabe (a retired lawyer recruited by Randy). The mayor told the chapter leaders, who had evolved from concerned citizens into seasoned leaders in the prior three years, that the support of Salem's Stand for Children was essential in order to pass an unprecedented 5% amusement tax that would fund a comprehensive middle school after-school program. As the mayor put it: "This is really a perfect Stand for Children issue. If you all don't take it on, it's not going to happen."

Jonah Edelman is the founder and executive director of Stand for Children. For more information on Stand for Children, visit www.stand.org.

Observing Children

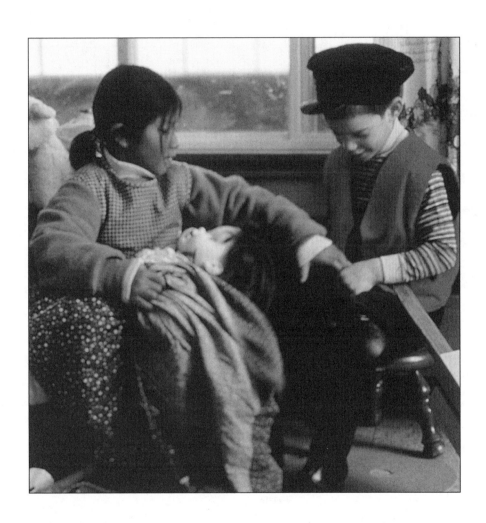

OBSERVING CHILDREN

Observation:
The Primary Tool in Assessment

by Kay (Stritzel) Rencken

"Most teachers want to know more about their students . . . what engages and interests them . . . we want to be more effective" (Ayres, 1993, p. 33). Observing and recording the behaviors of young children on a consistent basis helps to do this. Teachers will never know the complexity of the student but will have pieces of the puzzle — hopefully enough pieces so that a picture of the student emerges. Knowing children provides a way to chart the growth and plan for the learning to come.

Assessment, "the process of observing, recording, and otherwise documenting the work children do and how they do it, as a basis for a variety of educational decisions that affect the child, including planning for groups and individual children and communicating with parents . . . requires teachers to observe and analyze regularly what the children are doing in light of the content goals and the learning processes" (NAEYC, 1992, p. 10). NAEYC also lists the principles that should guide assessment for young children. An early childhood educator needs to be versed in these principles.

Learning to see the whole child

Observing young children requires the gathering of evidence of growth in a natural setting. An early childhood classroom is a familiar place where the child feels at ease in experimenting and exploring with blocks, various art media, writing, computers, puppets. This experimentation and exploration provides a rich storehouse of observable information for the teacher skilled in gleaning it from the play that surrounds the child. Observing in this setting looks at the whole child — not fragments or skills that are out of context. When a child is counting to see how many friends are at school today, there is authenticity; but when asked to count objects for a test, the reason is absent.

One of the important benefits of doing observations is that teachers are viewing many components at the same time. Unlike standardized tests, which focus only on cognition, observations allow the teacher to see the whole child. The emotional, physical, social, and cultural dimensions of the child are equally important, especially with the younger child.

Finding/making opportunities to observe

Early childhood teaching is a task that is filled with movement. Often teachers are doing ten tasks at the same time, moving from place to place, talking to children in the block, house, and writing centers. This view of perpetual motion pervades the profession. It is hard for many teachers to understand when they will find the time and how they can remain stationary and unobtrusive enough to observe the children. It requires a different mindset of the role of teaching young children. Observing and recording is just as crucial to good teaching as providing the setting, structuring the day, and planning the curriculum. Anne Benjamin (1993) gives many practical hints on how the teacher can effectively observe and record by planning what and when you observe, providing activities that don't directly involve the teacher, and having spots in the room that let teachers see and hear what is happening.

Teachers can also become skilled participant observers. They observe the development of a particular child or activity within the setting. These narrative observations often read like a story. They relate what happened during the day and are the basis for reflection and planning activities that will occur the next day. Teachers are full of stories of what happened in their room. These stories can be the basis of putting theory into practice or practice into theory as they are shared with other early childhood educators. These stories give voice to a group that has been silenced for far too long.

Keeping records of observations

Observing children often comes very easily. Teachers watch and remember what children are doing and how they accomplish the task. But observing without recording is only half of the picture. Teachers must find ways to keep all the information that they traditionally store in their heads. Insights are gained about who is being observed on a consistent basis. Stand-outs at either end of the spectrum are always remembered. Record keeping often reveals that some children are being observed more than the shy child or the invisible child or the child that is just minding to the business of playing and getting along. Careful records reveal information about the observer, such as preferences for certain centers of the room or certain times of the day. These insights offer the teacher an opportunity to broaden the perspective of the observations and record keeping.

Sharing observations with parents

Detailed records kept over time reveal growth in many areas. This can be shared with parents during formal and informal conferencing. Parents want to know more about their child's progress and they want to know that the teacher knows and understands their child. A good conference means that the adults are sharing the information about the growth and development of the child. It is a personal story that each shares with the other and is often done with laughter, concern, caring, and love. Most report cards and tests don't convey that the teacher really knows the child as good observational records do.

Using observations for planning

Detailed observational records are necessary to show the value of a curriculum that is based on children's needs. Planning begins with a knowledge of the age group and goals. Observation provides insights so that planning can be done to meet individual needs and evaluates the learning that takes place. Along the way, there are modifications made to meet individual and group needs and the cycle begins again.

Considering assessment

We are living in an era when early childhood educators are being asked to subject their children to all sorts of tests to determine a variety of information for a variety of purposes. Many of these are good tests, as tests go, but most of them subject a child to time spent away from learning so that someone can quickly determine what they have learned or not learned.

Often tests focus on what the child does not know. They are designed to show areas of weakness. Good observations focus on what the child knows and document areas of strengths.

Areas of concern are often closely linked to these strengths and are noted.

Many of the tests given to young children are not for their benefit but to:

■ help fund programs;

■ help train staff;

■ provide jobs for the testers and companies that make them; and

■ provide accountability statistics.

This is not to say that providing funds and training and accountability are necessarily bad, but there are other means of achieving the same results. Test results do not yield new information to the experienced observer.

Standardized testing is often not age appropriate. By definition, it is standardized and therefore for only a small portion of our children. Non-standardized tests are often very subjective. These tests and the time it takes to administer them are very costly.

Testing is very time consuming and takes time away from what a young child should be doing in a developmentally appropriate program. It also requires that time be spent after the testing to rebuild the child's self-esteem.

The issue of who administers the test is a two-edge sword. There is an ethical concern if the teacher is also the administrator of the test because, in testing lingo, she lacks the objectivity necessary. If an "outsider" who is unfamiliar to the child administers the test, the child probably will not be comfortable and will not perform as well.

These tests count for a disproportionate amount and matter a lot more to the adult than to the child. If funding or accountability are the reasons for a test, it matters more to the adult. If inclusion in gifted programs or a special preschool are the reasons, it matters more to the adult. Rarely does the test have meaning for the child.

Whenever there is widespread testing, there is also a phenomenon called "teaching to the test." This is not a new concept, but the fact that it is appearing in early childhood settings is new and alarming. Even the very best teachers who work to provide a play-based and developmentally appropriate setting are subject to this concept. Soon the test becomes the curriculum. This downward push of academic skills is not good early childhood education.

Early childhood educators are striving for professional recognition. In the past, we have had the view that we were not seen as "professional" as others. It was easy to cede the role of "expert" to people in other professions like psychologists, social workers, and physicians. They are experts in their field, but we are experts in ours! We know the children in our care because we observe them for many hours a day and watch how they react in a variety of settings, using many different tools, and working/playing with many different children and adults.

In order for teachers to resist the testing phenomenon, we must provide useful information about the growth and development of the children in our care. We must use our voices to articulate our observations as an integral tool of assessment in our classrooms. We must become proficient observers and recorders of the behaviors of young children. Observation is the root of all we do as teachers.

References

Ayres, W. (1993). *To Teach: The Journey of a Teacher.* New York: Teachers College Press.

Benjamin, A. C. (September 1993). "Observations in Early Childhood Classrooms: Advice from the Field." *Young Children,* 14-20.

Bentzen, W. R. (1985). *Seeing Young Children: A Guide to Observing and Recording Behavior.* Albany, NY: Delmar Publishers.

Boehm, A. E., & Weinberg, R. A. (1987). *The Classroom Observer: Developing Observation Skills in Early Childhood Settings.* New York: Teachers College Press.

Bredekamp, S., & Rosegrant , T. (editors). (1992). *Reaching Potentials: Appropriate Curriculum and Assessment for Young Children, Volume 1.* Washington, DC: NAEYC.

Bredekamp, S., & Rosegrant , T. (editors). (1995). *Reaching Potentials: Transforming Early Childhood Curriculum and Assessment, Volume 2.* Washington, DC: NAEYC.

Cohen, D. and V. Stern. (1978). *Observing and Recording the Behavior of Young Children.* New York: Teachers College Press.

Genishi, C. (1992). *Ways of Assessing Children and Curriculum.* New York: Teachers College Press.

Kamii, C. (1989). *Achievement Testing in the Early Grades: The Games Grown-Ups Play.* Washington, DC: NAEYC.

A retired kindergarten teacher and Pacific Oaks Adjunct Faculty who now volunteers in early childhood settings, works as a consultant and is active in SAzAEYC.

OBSERVING CHILDREN

To See Each Child with Wisdom, Humor, and Heart

by Sally Cartwright

"Learning is *experience*. The rest is information."
Einstein

This is true not only for children, but for each of us at work with them. Although we are guided by the findings of those who have gone before, our knowledge of each child will depend largely upon our own keen observation and recording, our own diligent and ever-lively experience with the children themselves.

10/10/95, 9:15, large block dramatic play area (names changed). Emily, aged four years and seven months (4.7), vigorously rolls an imaginary pie crust with an invisible roller. Ann, 4.1, having finally gotten her baby to sleep, comes over to chat. Suddenly Emily looks up, listening. She puts down her unseen roller, signs "wait" to Ann, and leaves her hastily-built kitchen. She slips by three painters at the wall easel, around the large unit block area, past Don driving nails into the nailing stump, past the 'cut, paste, and puzzles,' and onward to the reading corner, where she steps over two pairs of legs, whose small owners are busily "reading" a picture book together. Emily picks up a pretend phone, listens, nods, and lays the "receiver" down. She steps back over the legs and out of the reading corner, edges by the table work and Don's raised hammer, skirts the block area and the easels, returns to her kitchen, and says, "It's for you."

In a setting designed for child initiative guided by quiet, caring, adult authority, children actively learn at their own pace and style. This allows teachers and caregivers to watch and take notes on individual children, especially during creative, free-choice activities. It is in these child-centered ventures — and to youngsters they *are* adventures — that children most often reveal their own personalities and development.

Emily is no exception. She shows self-direction, concentration, and perseverance. But why was her kitchen hastily

built? That hardly seems her style. And what caused her protracted, single-minded intent on a phone call to a playmate? Since children of Emily's age are often more physical than verbal, to ask the child for answers not only intrudes but may invite frustration. Better to watch and interpret with wisdom, humor, and heart.

How can we best see and understand child behavior?

First of all, realizing the importance of observing and recording can motivate staff study and practice of the attitudes and skills needed for effective results. Why are recorded observations important? Anecdotal records not only raise questions for us to explore; they also point to answers. What do we know of Emily? We already have some answers: along with the three qualities mentioned above, we see that she can take the lead in dramatic play, and that she's certainly inventive and probably generous. As spot records accumulate, they are important for understanding the child.

Another reason for recorded observations is their use in staff meetings and parent conferences. Compared to generalizations, specific examples of child behavior speak with clarity, precision, and integrity. Staff members need to recognize this, and they need to know they have time for serious note-taking. Again, the school or child care environment which encourages child learning initiative and responsibility invites the adult to pause with respect for each child, to watch and listen, and, yes, to take notes. Nor will this observing and recording interfere with child learning.

On the contrary, keen adult interest shown by watching and recording is a boost to the child's self-esteem and purpose. When little Tom, curious about my note-taking, asked, "What you doing?" I said, "I really want to know how you kids learn, and I'm so interested I even write it down." He was satisfied.

Emily's anecdote demonstrates how immediate notation of an observation is far more accurate than memory. Regular staff members are *participant observers*, meaning that, while they are watching child behavior, they are very much part of the mix. When not actually leading the children, they guide the quality of child behavior simply by their presence. And that presence must consistently model caring, humor, respect, and integrity. Although no observer can be entirely objective, experienced observation and recording approach scientific methodology suitable for disciplined research (see Cohen & Stern, 1978). Those who perform at this level, who enjoy research as part of their professional work with children, often derive deep satisfaction from this extended insight and service to childhood. We can always learn more about child behavior through current research, our own as well as others. When those of us who work with children exhibit an inquiring mind, we model an important attitude for the children. The child who copies a loved and respected model employs a powerful way of learning.

How we record our observations is significant

There are various methods of recording, such as video filming, audio taping, and handwritten notes. Video filming is both intrusive and expensive. A participant observer can hardly wield a video camera without disturbing her child subjects. Some demonstration schools and centers have one-way screens to conceal the camera. I've worked with these in various settings, and find that concealing persons and procedure may stir child unease and mistrust. Using one-way screens to hide observers and cameras involves deceit. This feeling can permeate staff-child relationships and erode good learning. At all times, staff members need to be open and aboveboard with their children.

In my experience, audio taping tends to dull one's perceptions. When I tried a neat, almost invisible micro-taping device, I no longer tuned my ear to the children. Why should I, when it's all on tape anyhow? Furthermore, my occasional comments to the hidden recorder to explain the setting and name the children interrupted the children's play. Worst of all, both the children and I felt imposed upon by this mechanical contrivance which impaired our human rapport. Delicate adult-to-child relationships of affection, respect, guidance, and humor do not mesh with machines. Moreover, I had little time or patience for the necessary transcriptions. After many trials with mechanical equipment, I found that to understand and meet the needs of children the best method of all is on-the-spot note-taking by participant observers, teachers, and caregivers daily at work with these children.

There are numerous ways to take notes.

Some staff members use one or more 3" x 5" cards for each individual child, and later file them by date under the child's name. For many years, I've used a 6" x 9" spiral bound notebook, which I find easier to write on, to handle and not misplace, and easier for later reference. Pen and paper in whatever form should always be conveniently at hand.

I keep my notebook, precious as any personal journal, in a convenient, central location, out of sight and beyond reach. Notes about a named child are for professional use only. They are not to be shared with children, nor with parents or professionals who are not directly involved. Discretion must be used at all times. Confidentiality is essential for trust. Trust is essential for children.

When taking notes, as long as I do not disturb the children, I find it good to move discretely near my subjects so as to hear as much as possible. Depending on the children and the immediate situation, a casual or a friendly, supportive glance allows me to see and note their behavior without adverse influence. I do not try to hide my note-taking, because open honesty promotes good learning, and my obvious interest in the children's activity supports them.

Informed selection is imperative

A very important requirement for professional observation is a thorough knowledge of child development. One can neither see everything, nor record all that one sees. Informed selection is imperative. Teaching and child care professionals need a theoretical foundation to guide their choice of what to record. It will help them watch for behavior which depicts each child's stage of development and which hints of the unique qualities and potentials in each child.

A general knowledge of child development — for example, as in Stone and Church (1958), augmented, for example, by reading Piaget (1974), NAEYC's developmentally appropriate practice (Bredekamp, 1990), and the "developmental-interaction" approach to the child by Bank Street College of Education (see Boegehold, Cuffaro, Hooks, & Klopf, 1997; Biber, Shapiro, & Wickens, 1971; Shapiro & Biber, 1972; and DeVries & Kolberg, 1990) — provides a sound conceptual framework for observing and recording. The word *developmental* suggests a continuing, complex process of growth and learning, while *interaction* occurs between the child's emotional, physical, and cognitive growth, and between the child and her expanding physical and social environment. The stress is on *integrative* action by the children themselves.

The self of the observer is important

The last requirement for useful observation and recording is more subtle. I put it last because it refers not only to the process of observation and recording but to wise interpretation of the child's behavior and resulting adult action, if any. When a child care or teaching professional observes and selects child behavior for interpretation and acts on that interpretation, she must be not only informed, not only experienced, but well-balanced and mature.

As educational psychologist Barbara Biber (1948) said, she needs to be "so secure within herself that she can function with principles rather than prescriptions, that she can exert authority without requiring submission, that she can work experimentally but not at random, and that she can admit mistakes without feeling humiliated." These qualities are well chosen goals for each of us to emulate. They will help to ensure the wise, unbiased observation, recording, and resulting professional action that all children deserve. They will help to ensure our wisdom, humor, and heart.

References

Biber, B. (1948). *Childhood Education*. New York: Bank Street College of Education.

Biber, Shapiro, & Wickens. (1971). *Promoting Cognitive Growth from a Developmental-Interaction Point of View*. Washington, DC: NAEYC.

Boegehold, Cuffaro, Hooks, & Klopf. (1977). *Education Before Five*. New York: Bank Street College, 45-52.

Bredekamp, S. (editor). (1990). *Developmentally Appropriate Practice in Early Childhood Programs Serving Children from Birth Through Age 8* (Expanded Edition). Washington, DC: NAEYC.

Cohen, D. H., & Stern, V. (1978). *Observing and Recording the Behavior of Young Children* (Second Edition). New York: Teachers College Press, 2-3.

DeVries, R., & Kolberg, L. (1990). *Constructivist Early Education: Overview and Comparison With Other Programs*. Washington, DC: NAEYC.

Piaget, J. (1974). *The Language and Thought of the Child*. New York: American Library.

Shapiro, & Biber. (September 1972). "The Education of Young Children: A Developmental-Interaction Approach." *Teachers College Record*, Volume 74, Number 1.

Stone, L. J., & Church, J. (1958). *Childhood and Adolescence: A Psychology of the Growing Person*. New York: Random House.

Sally Cartwright, with an MS from Bank Street College of Education, has taught children and teachers across five decades. She has written eight books for children and much material on early childhood learning, especially as experienced in her own experimental school. She's still writing at 83.

OBSERVING CHILDREN

You've Got the Records —
Now What Do You Do with Them?

by Nancy Balaban

If you have kept your pad and pencil as steady companions and recorded one or two children over a period of time, engaged in varied activities, alone and with others, by now you have a treasured collection. You see the child in the process of learning to read, involved in math, block building after a social studies trip to the bakery, creating a book of stories, lining up, playing make-believe games, drawing, painting, arguing, and enjoying a joke. But now what?

Uses of records

Surely the most valuable use of these collected anecdotes is for the purpose of *teacher development*. You, the recorder, will benefit from knowing more about one particular individual, and in so doing you will know about other children. This knowing and understanding will have an impact on your behavior because you will see the child with new eyes. Here is an example of how a teacher gained a different view by recording a child she didn't like.

A teacher of seven year olds disliked the way Tim followed her and whined "teacher, teacher" many times during the day. The teacher was particularly repelled when Tim picked his nose and rolled the mucus into balls.

One day the teacher brought in sand and put out with fine, medium, and large mesh screens for the children to explore. The record she wrote of this small group using the sand contained Tim's words: "Hey, the sand comes out faster when the holes are larger!"

When she read the record aloud to colleagues, they called her attention to Tim's discovery. This teacher's prior judgment about Tim had prevented her from seeing the child's achievement.

Through observing and recording, you become a *researcher* in your own classroom. You will come to rely more confidently on yourself as a potent source of information. The records you take *will enhance your ongoing planning of curriculum* because you will be more keenly aware of the children's interests and abilities.

You can share what you've learned with colleagues and parents about the needs, the interests, the uniqueness, and the diversity of the children you live with daily in the classroom. You will share more than impressions or intuitions, you will have evidence on which to base your decision making.

But remember, no conclusion about a child is ever truly final. Just when you think you've figured out all about Susie or Tommy, zap! — they're on a new track. Written anecdotes provide concrete illustrations of the continually unfolding saga of development.

Sharing with staff

Records of a child provide a rich basis for meaningful staff meetings. The function of such record sharing is twofold. First, one or more staff members may be recording the same child over a period of time; and these shared anecdotes help staff understand not only the child in focus but some developmental characteristics of that specific age as well. Second, the very process of recording enriches staff development by serving as a basis for adult reflection about the refinements of their teaching practice. It is critical that the material in the records be *strictly confidential*. Use only the child's initial or a pseudonym, rather than her name in the sharing process.

Here is how one early child program uses records for their regular staff meetings. Each month one classroom team presents a child for study. (There are many reasons to choose a particular child to observe and record. Perhaps the child gets lost in the shuffle, and the staff wishes to know more; maybe the child gets along very well, and the staff wonders what the magic is;

perhaps the child's behavior is confusing, inconsistent, or aggressive.) Having made a choice, each member of the team — teacher, assistant, aide — takes records at every opportunity, making sure to include the date and time of each observation. The staff is careful *never to leave records lying around where others might see them.*

At the meeting the team organizes their recorded material by first describing the child's physical appearance, then the child's interests, the child's relations with other children and the teachers, the child's style of learning, the child's emotional tenor, the child's unique qualities, along with direct examples of speech. The team brings such artifacts as drawings, paintings, clay work, photo-graphs of block constructions, dictated or written stories, samples of math work. Specific examples from the observations are used throughout the presentation.

After the presentation, the whole staff asks questions and makes comments in order to get a fresh look at the child. The intent is not to "diagnose" but to elucidate, to bring the child more clearly into focus. Such sharing among and between staff members enables teachers to examine their own behavior and to make needed adjustments if necessary. The following anecdotes reveal as much about the teacher's behavior as the children's.

Bernard and Arturo (both four) are in the classroom loft shouting "Shut your mouth!" to each other. They each grab pillows and begin slamming them against one another. The teacher below says, firmly, "The loft is for quiet playing." Arturo drops his pillow, but Bernard jumps on top of Arturo and bangs him with the pillow several more times. The teacher climbs into the loft and plies Bernard off. Arturo climbs down. The teacher sits for several minutes talking quietly to Bernard, until he is able to reorganize himself and calmly climb down.

Omar (five) has just eaten a snack and left the spoon on the table. As he starts across the room, the teacher requests, "Omar, please put your spoon in the sink." "No!" he shouts, in an angry, loud voice. She holds his hand. He resists and lies on the floor pulling on her hand. She continues to hold his hand and quietly, but firmly, makes the request again. He lies on the floor for a few more minutes, glaring at her. Slowly he gets up, runs to the table, grabs the spoon, rushes across the room, and drops it in the sink. Respectfully, she says, "Thank you, Omar."

Sharing with parents

These observational records give authenticity to the conferences you hold with parents. In anticipation of a meeting with a parent, take records that document the child's interests, friendships, and approach to learning. In the course of the conference, examples from the records provide the specificity that supports an informational rather than judgmental tone. Parents appreciate such details that indicate how well you know their child.

Sharing with the next teacher

Records collected on a child or several children over the course of the year are useful in communicating with the child's next teacher. It is much more helpful to get a teacher's statement based on some actual documentation than on generalized statements such as "Janie is sweet and cooperative" or "Janie is impulsive and not at all cooperative." Making a short summary based on some of your observational records for the next teacher might look something like this:

Mia started out the year as shy and quiet. She only liked to look at books and play with the guinea pig. Little by little her friendship with Ashley and later with Drew seemed to draw her into new activities — painting, dramatic play, and finally blocks. She has been able to form a relationship with me and now comes to me when she needs help or when someone is "bothering" her. She is quite ready now to do more writing, story dictating, and experimenting with math materials.

Sharing with other professionals

Sometimes there are children about whom you have special concerns, because their behavior has been *often* and *consistently* unusual or puzzling over a period of time. You may wish to obtain the help of a mental health professional. Having a series of observational records taken over a period of several weeks or months will focus attention on the history of that child in your group.

An alternative to testing

Studying children at play and at work in early childhood classrooms is becoming a viable alternative to standardized achievement tests. Many national educational organizations have called for a halt to formalized assessments of children under age eight because the tests have not been considered valid measures of children's learning. The largest early childhood organization in the country, the National Association for the Education of Young Children (NAEYC) has issued guidelines for assessing young children. Assessment is defined as:

[To] provide an accurate picture of children's capabilities, teachers must observe children over time. . . . Assessment relies primarily on procedures that reflect the ongoing life of the classroom and typical activities of the children . . . [it] utilizes an array of tools . . . including . . . work by children (artwork, stories they write, tape recordings of their reading), records of systematic observations by teachers, records of conversations and interviews with children, teachers' summaries of children's progress as individuals and as groups. (NAEYC & NAECS/SDE, 1991, p. 32)

Observing and recording — tools for good early childhood practice

The records you make will lead you to improve your teaching through the process of examining your own behavior as well as by sharing your records with others and by getting to know the children in your group as individuals and group members. You will be able to step aside from your own point of view to see children *as they are*. These records will also help you understand children whose culture is different from your own. Observing and recording helps all teachers refine their practice by getting closer to the children they teach.

Reference

National Association for the Education of Young Children and the National Association of Early Childhood Specialists in State Departments of Education (NAEYC & NAECS/SDE). (1991). "Guidelines for Appropriate Curriculum Content and Assessment in Programs Serving Children Ages 8 Through 18." *Young Children*, 46, (3), 21-38.

Nancy Balaban is the former director of the Infant and Parent Development and Early Intervention Program and Bank Street Graduate School of Education in New York City. Presently she teaches courses and advises students in fieldwork. Author of the recently published *Everyday Goodbyes:Starting School and Early Care: A Guide to the Separation Process*, she is currently working as co-author on the fifth editon of *Observing and Recording the Behavior of Young Children* by Dorothy Cohen, Virginia Stern, and Nancy Balaban. Both books are published by Teachers College Press.

Observations Are Essential in Supporting Children's Play

by Gretchen Reynolds

It is midmorning during free play time. The blocks scattered around on the floor of the block building area are evidence that children played here earlier. Four quadruple unit blocks (Hirsch, 1984) or "quads" have been placed together in the shape of a large square. Checking out the block building area, four year olds Jennifer and Rosie notice it immediately. The girls help themselves to unit and half unit blocks and begin filling in the big, empty square.

Jennifer: Wanna make something in here?

Rosie: Yeah!

Jennifer: We're making roads. We're making roads for putting in everywhere.

As she passes by, a teacher calls: What are you girls building?

Rosie: A car road.

Jennifer: It's not for racing. It's not a racing road. It's a regular road.

Jennifer and Rosie systematically place unit blocks around the inside edge of the square to form a border all the way around. (Four unit blocks equal a quad.) Then, using units and half unit blocks, they fill in from all four sides toward the center. (Two half unit blocks equal one unit block, or eight half units equal a quad.) Because all the blocks they use are mathematical equivalents, the girls are creating a patterned mosaic floor inside the square. During this fill-the-square activity, a quad on one side is bumped, slightly distorting the square shape.

Now only one row, three units long, remains empty. Jennifer places a unit block in the middle of it, leaving space for a half unit on one side, and a small undefined hole on the other side. At this point she seems stuck: she pushes the unit block to the left and to the right in an attempt to figure out what will fill the space. But Jennifer does not notice that the square itself is slightly misshapen. Then Rosie hands

Jennifer a small plastic car, and the girls begin "driving" the cars counterclockwise around the floor of the square.

Jennifer: This is a car one, and this is a car one.

Jennifer points out the oddly shaped hole to Rosie: That's where you park. Come this way and this way and come over and park.

Rosie: That's the jail.

Jennifer puts her car in the hole, and slides the unit block to fill up the space.

Then, almost as quickly as they came, the girls get up to leave the block building area.

Why watch play?

The observation of Jennifer's and Rosie's block building play comes from a recent video recording. Video cameras are useful in obtaining accurate records of classroom events that can be replayed any number of times. I try to be sensitive to children's reactions to the camera, and I turn it off if I get a message from a child that it feels intrusive.

Play-watching is essential; video cameras are not. A teacher may prefer to carry a small notebook in a pocket, or to keep paper and pencils handy. When a teacher pauses to watch play, she should record the action and children's language in detail, being careful to identify the players, the time of the day, and the place of the play.

The episode of Jennifer's and Rosie's block building play lasted just five minutes. To get a good observation, a teacher does not need to record a long time. The amount of time to record can be guided by the play itself, rather than by the clock. Episodes of play flow like a story, with a clear beginning, middle, and end. Just as the children do, play-watchers know when an episode of play is finished.

I am a committed watcher of children's play, and for me almost every observation evokes teaching questions — questions that usually do not have easy answers. Notes carefully jotted or video clips of incidental play contain the clues to a child's well-being and, when thoughtfully examined, the stimulus for effective teaching.

When I observed Jennifer's and Rosie's block building play, and viewed it again on the video recording, I was taken by the elaborate tessellation they conjured inside that large square shape. They were master builders! But I found myself wondering: Could their play be more satisfying if they had figured out how to fill in the empty row? Would a teacher disrupt their play if she intervened to point out the skewed quad that they did not seem to notice? When does a teacher's intervention interrupt play and when does it support sustained involvement?

Play is a developmental task of early childhood. Stretching their skills in construction play and dramatic play, "patterners" and "dramatists" (Wolf & Gardner, 1979) play to get better at it, and they play to learn.

Play is the child's natural way of learning; it provides the time and opportunities children need to construct their own knowledge. Play poses an appropriate cognitive challenge as children use it in shaping social and physical worlds still unpredictable for them. Young children represent their experiences and feelings through play, entering into the long human tradition of symbol-making in order to know. (Reynolds & Jones, 1997)

Early childhood programs that support the child's potential to engage her skills in play are a good fit for young children. Teachers know if their interventions in children's play — and that includes deciding not to intervene — have been supportive of children's growth when they see competence, sustained involvement, and mastery of play.

Teachers as theory-builders

By watching children's play and reflecting on the roles of teachers in supporting master players, teachers' skills grow (Jones & Reynolds, 1992). Writing thoughts in a journal or keeping notes in a file on the computer are two private ways that effective teachers reflect on children's play and their teaching practice.

Reflective practice can also be collaborative: a team of teachers my find that fruitful discussions happen when observations are shared in a climate of trust. When reflecting on an observation of play, teachers sometimes invent their own questions.

Or — here are some suggestions:

■ What is the child's (children's) agenda?

■ Is this a valuable way for the child to be spending his time?

■ Is this child a master player or master building? How do I know?

■ What are the roles of the teacher in supporting this child's play?

Curious about how others would respond to Rosie's and Jennifer's block building play, and wanting to test the idea that teachers can learn from each other through collaborative reflection, I asked three colleagues to watch the videotape and discuss it.

Here is a condensed version of their dialogue.

Leigh: They were really taking turns, and sharing the blocks, and working together. And I thought it was really neat the way they took the blocks and fitted them all the way around 'til everything fit right in like a puzzle, without changing the shape of the outside. It would be interesting to see if Jennifer likes puzzles or working with tangrams.

Kathy: What interested me was the way Jennifer kept fiddling with the space that was left in the center. She started to fill it in with a block, but because the shape they were filling was a little uneven to begin with, she saw that the block in her hand didn't quite fit. She put another block in one side, but she kept trying to squish them together different ways to fill that hole in. Then she started saying they were in jail.

Leigh: As a teacher, I would have gotten more involved.

Leslie: But do you think involvement by a teacher would have interfered with the play?

Kathy: A teacher might interfere, or she could extend what they're playing.

Leigh: I wonder why they were playing cars. They seemed like piddly little cars. They were the kind you get in the bottom of cereal boxes or at a fast food drive-in.

Leslie: The dramatic play with the cars wasn't all that fascinating anyway. But the girls were doing some of the math on their own, without having help from an adult. Right at the beginning, when Jennifer took a rectangular block, she realized the hole required a square. So she gave Rosie the square and showed her where to put it.

Kathy: If I were the teacher, I'd want to reinforce their block building in some way. Because that was some good play, but it did not hold their interest for very long.

Leigh: How many times do you look at a brick wall or cobblestone sidewalk, and you never notice the different patterns of the brick? What bothered me was there was an incredible amount of math going on inside that square, and nobody drew their attention to it. I wonder if a teacher could have asked some questions, at the risk of interrupting them, to get them to pay attention to the pattern they had created, and to see if they wanted to complete it. It reminded me of parquetry floor, but with a big hole in it! I had the feeling "it's not complete!" With that hole they left I had no sense of closure.

Leslie: But Jennifer was looking around for a block to fill it. Her good imagination made it into a jail, which is interesting.

Leigh: But not as interesting as a patterned floor. They really were more interested in building than in playing with cars. Their building was really quite lovely.

Kathy: So you think it was more construction play than dramatic play?

Leslie: Yes. And I think they would eventually have thought of a way to fill up that hole, but for the time being they saw some other interesting ways to use that hole.

Leigh: I thought the cars were way too small. I would have gotten some other props to encourage dramatic play, like road signs, you know the lovely wooden road signs that say "stop," and "railroad crossing," and "bike" path.

Kathy: Do you think if they had more props they would have lost focus on the math aspects of their play? Because it's play, generally we don't even talk about math. We don't even ask "How many blocks are in here?" or "If you filled up this hole, what would you get?" or "Is there a way you could fill in this hole?"

Leslie: Do you need to direct them that much? Instead could you ask them some questions that might get them to start thinking about it?

Leigh: What would be a good question, if you don't want to interrupt their play?

Kathy: I think we use that as a crutch, that we don't want to "interrupt." And in the meantime a lot of good play goes unnoticed or gets no support because teachers believe in a hands-off approach.

Leslie: You can ask them to tell you about it, or comment that it's an interesting pattern, but don't make them count the blocks. That could stifle the play. They're into filling up that space by pretending it's a jail, and now they've got to count the blocks?

Kathy: They can always ignore you!

Leigh: You could get paper, and trace over the top! Or even do a rubbing to see the pattern!

Kathy: Or extend the idea outdoors, to look at the brick designs in the walkways.

Leslie: Maybe they were interested in dramatic play, but those cars were just not right. A teacher could make a comment like, "They seem to be getting stuck in the cracks." Then maybe you could encourage some problem solving by asking, "Are there some cars that we could get that would work better on this car road?" They might have been interested in driving cars around in a spiral like the Indy 500.

Leigh: They weren't involved for very long. Maybe if a teacher did observe that block building, she could even do something the next day to encourage more in-depth play.

Kathy: Also the block building area was way too small. How do you have "real" roads in such a small space?

Leigh: How about setting up that road the next day, and bringing out other props, and waiting to see what would happen? And fill in the hole, and see if anybody noticed? Or make a new pattern or some different shapes?

Kathy: It could also be a conversation piece at the lunch table that day, to talk about what you saw in the morning in block building. I wonder who put it away? Wouldn't it be neat to leave it there, not clean it up, and add on to it later, after nap?

In this discussion, Leslie, Kathy, and Leigh did not resolve the question of whether the girls' agenda was construction play or dramatic play, or if intervention by a teacher would support it or interrupt. But by engaging in mutual reflection, they considered what the children were learning in their play and the different possibilities for action by a teacher to support more complex play.

If teachers were to have conversations like this in weekly team meetings, with the goal of reflecting on their teaching practice collaboratively, they could construct effective ways of supporting children's master play and develop their skills as teachers. Collaborative reflection like this empowers teachers as theory-builders.

Reality-based teaching

While teachers' different perspectives will generate lively dialogue about the play, and discussions can move in unpredictable ways, the goal is not necessarily convergence. Through dialogue, teachers will collaboratively construct understandings about the children's needs and interests and strategies for teaching interventions that effectively support children's play, growth, and learning. This teaching practice is reality-based, because it is grounded in the teachers' own observations of the children they care for.

Teaching is a challenging enterprise because children are always changing. Effective teachers also change. Teaching practice that is a good fit for the growing child is based on ongoing observations of play, reflection, hypothesis generation and testing, and evaluation. Teachers ". . . must accept and reject ideas on the basis of thoughtful inquiry and not just on the basis of superficial opinion, private belief, or standard practices. Teachers need to recognize that teaching is a complex, professional activity requiring constant effort on their part." (Bowman & Stott, 1994, p. 129)

References

Bowman, B. T., & Stott, F. M. (1994). "Understanding Development in a Cultural Context: The Challenge for Teachers." In B. Mallory and R. New (editors), *Diversity and Developmentally Appropriate Practices: Challenges for Early Childhood Education*. New York: Teachers College Press.

Hirsch, E. S. (editor). (1984). *The Block Book*. Washington, DC: NAEYC.

Jones, E., & Reynolds, G. (1992). *The Play's the Thing: Teachers' Roles in Children's Play*. New York: Teachers College Press.

Reynolds, G., & Jones, E. (1997). *Master Players: Learning from Children at Play*. New York: Teachers College Press.

Wolf, D., & Gardner, H. (1979). "Style and Sequence in Early Symbolic Play." In B. Smith and M. Franklin (editors), *Symbolic Functioning in Childhood*, 117-138. Hillsdale, NJ: Erlbaum.

Gretchen Reynolds is a full-time faculty member in the Early Childhood Education Program at Algonquin College in Ottawa, Ontario, and an adjunct faculty member at Pacific Oaks College in Pasadena, California.

Collaboration

COLLABORATION

Facilitatiing Collaborations Among Children

by Susan Stacey

Tara watches from her wheelchair as her preschool peers tear around the playground. Her paraprofessional, Liz, provides playthings and is engaged with her, but Tara is watching the other children play with the wagons. Liz notices the other children's interest in pulling the wagons along the bike trail and calls to them, "Hey, would you like a ride?" Several would, and they approach Liz and Tara. Turning the wheelchair around to face the wagon, Liz puts the handle in Tara's hand. She has a tight grip, and pulls two children around the bike path. Another child with a second wagon notices this, comes over, and holds on to the first wagon. The train-like vehicle is pulled around the bike path for 45 minutes.

As a teaching team, we at Purdue University's Child Development Lab School were inspired by this collaboration between children, and the facilitation that occurred in order to make it happen. When planning the beginning of our school year, the team had been aware that the children in this group (20 children of mixed ages between three and five years, with about 50 percent English language learners and four children with special needs) would need a great deal of support in order to form collaborative relationships.

My belief was that collaboration was crucial to the development of self-esteem, problem-solving, and negotiation skills, and that it would foster respect between children. So, as well as providing for a stimulating atmosphere and curriculum, we also planned to start our year by setting up the environment to encourage collaboration: two easels side by side so children could talk about what they were doing, small spaces for two or three children to work together, toys in the sandbox that required three hands — and thus the help of a friend — to manipulate. The curriculum itself would emerge as the children engaged with materials and each other, and we would spend the first two or three weeks building rapport and routines as the children got to know their peers and their teachers.

What we were not prepared for were the barriers that our many languages produced: children with shared language formed their own groups and did not willingly mix with others. We did not understand their conversations and therefore could not easily support their efforts during play. The children with special needs were often isolated due to lack of communication skills on the part of almost all of the children.

Yet, we observed some collaboration occurring during everyday routines: one child who spoke both English and Mandarin would translate for the other Mandarin-speaking child, a child with a communication disorder was adept at helping other children find a missing item, a child who spoke Korean noticed an older English-speaking child struggling to carry a ladder in the playground and silently came to assist. Language, it seemed, may be a barrier to forming typical friendships, but was not a barrier to collaborative, helping behaviors.

Building upon collaborative behaviors

We asked ourselves in those first weeks what we could do to support and extend these naturally-occurring collaborations. As a head teacher, I was occasionally able to leave the room and observe from an observation booth. What I noticed was that sometimes adults were stepping in when children could have successfully helped each other or worked together. For example, struggles with zippers were always handled by an adult; a teacher would pass the basket around at snack time, organize turn-taking (especially during disputes!), or look for needed materials.

Our belief was that the children's feelings of competence would be enhanced if they were collaborating on these everyday problems and also collaborating with teachers in performing meaningful tasks pertaining to the upkeep of their environment. From my own work in Montessori, High/Scope, and Reggio-inspired classrooms, I knew that the children's input into the care of the environment and their collaboration in determining the direction of activities and projects would lead to a more child-centered space and an emergent curriculum. Having recognized that sometimes adults could intervene too much, our next step was to think about standing back while still supporting children. How to do this while still scaffolding children's learning? This, and many other questions, surfaced over the fall semester.

More questions and discussion:

The Lab School is blessed with an abundance of enthusiastic, well-educated, and energetic staff, students, and therapists. It seemed obvious to both the teaching staff and the coordinator for children with special needs that all of us needed to keep our goals in mind if collaboration was to be enhanced. Therefore, we began thinking about new approaches:

■ Could the student participants, therapists, student teachers, and teaching staff be asked to take a moment to look around before responding to a child's "I can't do this?" Could another child collaborate, rather than a teacher helping? If not, to what degree should the teacher assist? This became a question of great debate. The children's needs must, of course, be met. But were we doing too much for them? How could other children help solve the problem?

■ Could the environment be changed to further facilitate collaboration? We had already changed some areas of the room . . . what else could we do?

■ Could a buddy system help in some way, both with typically-developing children and those with special needs?

■ How could the language barriers be addressed?

■ In addition to helping behaviors, could children also be collaborators in terms of decisions about curriculum? This was an approach that I had experimented with at a previous workplace, and I was familiar with audiotaping children's conversations, analyzing them, and developing curriculum from this input. Could this be used in the present setting, considering the level of diversity we were working with?

Actions taken:

Toward the end of the semester, through a great deal of trial and error — which we now refer to as teacher research — several new approaches were implemented:

■ During a particularly hectic daily transition, we paired children into book buddies, the idea being that they would look at books together, and in the process collaborate in English language-learning. This meant that children had to be paired strategically — an English-speaking child with an English language learner. We did this by placing two carpet squares together, placing the children's name cards on them, and providing one book.

■ We took a very critical look at our environment and routines, trying to see them through new eyes. We put tables together so that two chairs fit onto each side. We lowered easel paper so that children could reach it, and provided clothespins so one child could hold the paper while another pinned it to the easel. Children were sent in pairs or small groups to wash their hands in preparation for snack, with those needing help being paired with those who could give it. We changed our helpers chart (jobs that children did around the classroom) to one that allowed children to work together on these simple tasks, such as cleaning the guinea pig cage or watering flowers.

■ We tackled the issue of too much help from staff. When meeting with paraprofessionals, speech and language athologists, students and volunteers, we explained our rationale and asked that, whenever possible, they encourage all children to help each other, share ideas, and work together. We suggested that they take a few seconds to look around and see what other children were doing before responding to a request for teacher assistance. As well, we requested that only one professional at a time work with children with special needs, and that they always try to involve the other children in their activities so that the child was surrounded by his or her peers rather than by adults.

■ We brainstormed ways that children could work together outside: building tents, pulling heavy items, playing cooperative games, and using traffic signs on the bike path.

■ We were already committed to the philosophy of children as co-constructors of curriculum, and pledged to work more actively to make this happen. We prepared to take more photographs of children working together, to have children talk together about these photographs, and to audiotape their conversations to provide an opportunity for curriculum to emerge from their thoughts and ideas. We had a vision of an environment where there was shared control and collaboration rather than the "Teacher as Expert."

■ Following up on the children's developing interest in print, we set up a writing area that would allow a quiet space for children to dictate stories, act out favorite plots, send messages to each other and to teachers, and use flannelboards together.

What happened:

While some of these ideas are still in the process of implementation, others have proven to be extremely successful. Following are some observations of the children at work together:

In a quiet, carpeted area, a child with cerebral palsy is stretching, reluctantly, with his paraprofessional. Another child is watching, and is invited to join in. He lies down on the floor and the children do stretches together. The child with special needs thinks this is great fun and breaks into a wide smile. He becomes more cooperative and enthusiastic about his stretches.

Adam, a child who is learning English and who has a strong sense of story, tells me a brief story during play while I take dictation: "One people lived with her Mom. Then she planted a seed. The tree grow up. Then the winter came, the tree fall down." At circle time, I plan for us to act out familiar nursery rhymes for the first time. This goes well, so I produce Adam's story, and we act this out too. Other children want to tell stories, and so later in the afternoon this becomes an added activity.

Children, provided with envelopes and a mailbox, begin to send "messages" to each other and to teachers. I ask a child to take a message to a teacher across the room, and she chooses to write the message rather than deliver it verbally. Children negotiate who will deliver the mail, and how.

We support student teachers as they learn to "go with the flow" at circle time. That is, when the children have an idea to act out, sing, or play, the student is encouraged and supported in letting go of the original plan and responding to the children's agenda. This is, at first, a frightening action to take — somewhat like stepping off a precipice, but the results are worth it. We see a heightened responsiveness from the children and a greater level of participation.

We implement the book buddy idea. The children, at first, strenuously object to being paired with someone not of their own choosing. However, after about three days, we see a change. The pairs are working well together, and even though they do not share language, the children communicate by pointing at illustrations and gesturing. They begin to pick up on each other's language, repeating single words and laughing.

As early childhood educators, we know that collaboration is a valuable tool for children to take into the world. At the Lab School, we continue to think about ways of increasing collaboration between children and between children and teachers. The children have shown us that they are able to engage in this process in the preschool years, no matter what their language or ability. We can think about children collaborating when someone needs help, when an idea for play becomes stuck, or when there is a problem to be solved. We can include their input when planning curriculum. They are capable of doing this — we simply have to offer them the chance.

Susan Stacey is a head teacher at Purdue University's Laboratory Preschool. She has worked in the field of early childhood education for 24 years and has previously worked in Halifax, Nova Scotia, as a director, instructor, practicum supervisor, and program coordinator. Susan and her husband Brian recently moved to the United States and live in West Lafayette, Indiana.

COLLABORATION

One Size Doesn't Fit All — Collaborations With Parents

by Deborah E. Eaton

As we move into a new century, we must rethink the established standard of working with parents, a one-size-fits-all mentality, and embrace a new model of collaboration where one size fits some but certainly not all of our children and families. This follows every tenet we hold sacred in early childhood, including the uniqueness of each child and family.

Collaborations with parents must change because the nature of today's family has changed. We have dual-parent families, single-parent families, stepfamilies, blended families, and grandparents and other extended family members raising children. We have adopted families, foster families, families with two mommies, and families with two daddies. We also have families with different cultural and linguistic needs. I think it is safe to say that we have many different kinds of parents and families with many different kinds of needs.

Accepting and respecting differences is at the very core of collaborating with parents. Each and every parent who walks through our doors will have a different set of values, beliefs, goals, customs, and needs. We will be able to identify with some of these differences but not all of them. Our challenge as early childhood professionals will be to establish a common ground that will allow us to work together to establish a basis for understanding and communication.

In a child care setting we will observe many different kinds of parenting. It is imperative that we observe without judging or labeling parents. We must be sensitive to the fact that each parent has good intentions. How parenting is done is a very complex process, determined by what was modeled by their own parents, their personal philosophies, and level of parent education.

Building collaborations

One of the most important elements in building collaborations with parents is to have open communication at all times. We can do this by having frequent communication with parents, informing them of activities, asking for their suggestions and feedback, and communicating any problems as they arise.

Another important aspect of communication with parents is to be positive whenever possible. Parents will listen more attentively when we're telling them something positive about their child. If we only communicate negative situations, many parents may never put forth the effort to truly hear or understand us.

When parents of young children work, they often miss their child's developmental milestones . . . first tooth, first step, learning to skip, or learning to tie their shoes, etc. This is not uncommon given the fact that we are often with children the majority of their waking hours. One of the things we can do as teachers is to not steal those milestones from parents. Let them be the ones to tell us about these important events, then celebrate together.

Parental guilt and fears

America has become a society where everyone is expected to work, even parents with young children. Many parents have to work out of economic necessity. Because of this, some parents may experience guilt for having left their children in the care of others. Other parents may fear that their children will be injured or that their children will care for their teachers more than them.

We need to understand parental guilts and fears in order to understand a parent's interactions with staff. Sometimes these feelings manifest themselves in bizarre and unpredictable behaviors such as being cold or distant, denying problems, or even treating a staff member as an employee instead of a partner.

For example, a parent may feel guilty for not being able to take time off from work to accompany the child's group on field trips or to volunteer in the program. Perhaps another kind of assistance may be done at home or on the weekend that would be just as valuable to the success of a program. We must think of alternative ways for today's busy parents to be a part of the program. This facilitates not only parental pride but parental partnerships.

Before we can help parents work through their guilts and fears, we must first examine our own beliefs about working parents. We must accept the fact that everyone has the right to work outside the home, whether it's because they have to work or because they choose to have a career. Developing an understanding of these guilts will enable us to not take actions personally and therefore avoid escalating a situation into a full-blown conflict. If we can view parental behaviors objectively, we will foster more opportunities for true collaborations to take place. Remember that it will be the child who will benefit from the efforts put forth to understand.

Collaborations for consideration

We recently did an informal poll of the parents in our program to find out what they felt were the most successful collaborations we have partnered in for their children. The results were much of what we felt they would say. However, there were a few surprises.

The number one response received was communication based. Parents really like to sit down with their child's teacher to discuss the child's individual developmental goals. Many programs do this on an annual, biannual, or a quarterly basis. There is current debate surrounding the assessment of our children and how it relates to performance measures of our programs. Nonetheless, practitioners' perspectives and parent voices should play an important role in both kinds of assessments.

We use a simple system to receive ongoing parental feedback about their child. We have a dedicated space on the daily sign-in sheet to list any information we may need to know about their child for the day, along with any concerns they may have. When a comment is written, they receive feedback from our program. This feedback makes them feel respected and lets them know that their comments are taken seriously by us.

Parents also like to receive frequent information about their child's activities. There are many ways to do this. Some programs send home a daily note about what they have done; others send home a weekly letter; still others send home a monthly newsletter and calendar. On a write-on/wipe-off board, we list the activities for the day along with the meals and snacks served.

We also send home a monthly newsletter that gives an overview of the developmental goals for the upcoming month. The newsletter also lists special days such as Red Day (wear something red) or Teddy Bear Day (bring your favorite bear) in addition to any days the program will be closed. In order to reinforce the monthly newsletter, we also send home a quarterly parent calendar listing the days the program will be closed during that quarter.

Because we have a mixed-age group, we do individual daily notes for each child 12 months or younger. It has been our experience that parents of babies need to know greater daily details about their child — for example, when they have napped and for how long, when and what they have eaten and how much, and, of course, their frequency of diaper changes.

The use of technology has expanded the possibilities for communication with many of today's families. Many programs are now using the Internet to both send and receive information from parents. Some have even installed on-line video cameras where program activities may be viewed from a parent's home, library, or workplace during certain hours of the day.

Another frequently mentioned area of collaboration with parents is that of toilet learning. This is probably one of the areas where the facilitation of partnering is essential in order to achieve the desired results. Collaboration for toilet learning is twofold and will come as no surprise. First, the child must be physically and developmentally ready for the experience. Second, the parents must be equally ready to follow through when the child is at home. In fact, many programs require that the parents begin the process at home before the process is begun in the program.

We expected parents to talk about partnering with us concerning taking care of mildly ill children, and they did. Communication is once again a factor as we define what constitutes mildly ill and what constitutes when the child must not come or should be immediately picked up. Parents must also be made aware of the program's policy regarding the giving of any medications.

One surprise was the frequency that parents mentioned collaborations concerning nutritional guidelines. Of course, great care is taken to gather information about a child's food allergies or specific nutritional requirements, but we also gather information about the foods that are customarily eaten in the home. Children really like to talk about the food groups, their personal favorites, shopping, and preparation.

Parents like to know what their child is served each day (this sometimes prevents the same foods being served for the child's meal at home) and if they are eating the foods served that are new to them. One of our favorite projects is to do an annual cookbook consisting of each child's favorite recipe. Some programs may do this and even sell the cookbooks as a fundraiser. Regardless of the distribution, this is a hit with children and parents alike.

Another collaboration that was mentioned by the parents had to do with the issues surrounding child guidance. When there is a consistency of guidelines (at home and in your program) for acceptable and unacceptable behaviors, children feel more secure. There is also the added benefit of sharing with the parent our rationale for the guidance used. By facilitating this type of sharing, we often reap the benefit of being able to model for less experienced parents appropriate ways to guide or redirect inappropriate behaviors.

Other areas that were mentioned included bartering with parents for either goods needed for your program or for services to be rendered. For example, one program is having a room added in lieu of weekly tuition for a set number of weeks. Another area of possible collaboration might be in the occasional scheduling of early drop off or late pick up.

As you can see, there are many areas where parent collaborations are both desirable and necessary for the smooth and optimal operation of your program. And like anything worthwhile, effort is required to achieve the desired results. Getting back to that one-size-fits-all mentality . . . I hope you can see that there are a myriad of options available for collaboration with parents. One size definitely does not fit all!

Many parents work long, hard days (just like we do). They may also work with hostile or unpleasant adults while we spend our day in the company of children. If we want parents to understand our needs and those of their children, we must be sensitive to their needs. How hard is it and how much time does it really take to inquire about what they do, to ask what kind of day they have had? We must keep in mind that we care for families, not just children.

Deborah Eaton, past president of the National Association for Family Child Care (NAFCC), lives in San Diego and has been working with young children and their families for the past 25 years. She currently serves as director of accreditation for the National Association for Family Child Care Foundation. Deborah also serves as a consultant to parents, child care providers, and to state and local early childhood administrators. She was recently appointed as representative for the Americas by t he International Family Child Care Association at the 1999 conference in Glasgow, Scotland.

COLLABORATION

Supporting Collaboration Among Teachers

by Kay Albrecht

Collaboration among teachers isn't a new idea. Good teachers have always collaborated — as a strategy for solving problems, reducing isolation, finding others with like interests or concerns, and validating or celebrating successes in the classroom. Alternately called mentoring, coaching, reflecting, and even sometimes, problem-solving, collaboration is considered a successful strategy for preventing the isolation of teachers, supporting beginning teachers, reducing teacher turnover, improving the quality of care and early education, and supporting professional development of experienced teachers (Love & Rowland, 1999).

Attention is being given to collaboration in our professional literature and in practice, primarily because teacher educators are recognizing its potential for improving the education of teachers in training and helping new teachers succeed. Collaboration as a strategy for supporting teachers as they learn and grow shares in a way that enriches the learning experience for all involved.

Some kinds of collaboration are formal in nature — set up for a specific purpose; other kinds are informal — emerging from the relationships that develop in schools among teachers, directors, parents, and the community. Whether formal or informal, collaboration can be very powerful. The teachers in the programs of Reggio Emilia value the collaboration process so much that it is considered one of the most crucial roles of the teacher (Gandini, Edwards, & Forman, 1998; 1993). Although collaboration among children, parents, directors or supervisors, and specialists are important as well, this article focuses on collaboration among teachers.

Although some collaborations happen spontaneously, most are carefully planned and nurtured. Further, there are prerequisites that support collaboration. According to Tertell, Klein, & Jewett (1998), collaboration emerges when teachers:

■ trust and respect each other

■ have time to be together to talk, discuss, and reflect

■ have worked to develop communication skills

■ discover common ground (concerns, interests, needs, goals)

■ are supported in the reflection process

The exciting thing about this list is that teachers can create these characteristics. Then they can use collaborations to inform and improve their teaching practice. This is professional development at its best. It is tied to individual teaching needs; occurs when the collaborators are interested in the idea, topic, or skill; and is under the control of the participants rather than controlled by an external trainer or teacher educator.

Types of collaboration

Some types of collaboration are connected to the structure and function of the school. These are usually planned, not incidental, experiences. They are a part of the thoughtful process of designing a work climate that views teachers as an integral part of the success of the school and creates roles and experiences for them that validate this view.

Others types of collaboration are interactive experiences. Interactive collaboration can be spontaneous, real-time events — opportunities for teachers to connect and support one another as they interact during the school day. Or, they can be planned experiences that are designed to facilitate collaboration among teachers.

Where does collaboration begin?

Most agree that collaboration cannot be forced or assigned. The nature of collaboration is the voluntary participation of the participants. Nor are perfect work environments necessary for collaboration to occur. In fact, collaborations that occur early in teaching careers are usually around negative experiences or unsuccessful teaching attempts. When these occur, new teachers quickly look for support and help to, for example, validate their feelings or to get ideas about what else to try.

Some examples of collaboration among teachers

Participating in recruiting and selecting colleagues. When teachers collaborate to recruit and select their colleagues, the results can be very powerful. Teachers within programs are usually able to tell whether applicants are good matches for the program. Teachers can also help applicants determine if the program is a good fit for their skills and interest.

Orienting new teachers. Collaboration among experienced and new teachers in the orientation process is a win/win situation. Every teacher remembers how hard it is to get in and get started in a new school. Further, feeling welcome and appreciated helps new teachers make important connections at work that enhance their feelings of success.

Peer, mentor, and technical coaching. These three types of coaching (Scanlon, 1988) are the heart of collaborations. Examples of the range of roles peer, mentor, and technical coaches use include listening, observing, analyzing the teaching strategies being used by a teacher, offering emotional support, encouragement for resolving interpersonal conflicts, organizing space or materials, "teaching" a new skill, giving advise, demonstrating techniques, encouraging attempts to try new ideas, copying useful materials and references, discussing relevant literature, examining children's work together, choosing a mutual topic for learning, and so forth (Carter, 1998; Love & Rowland, 1999).

Visitations and observations. Seeing is believing for many early childhood teachers. Visitations and observations broaden and enrich teachers' experiences. Visits can be to other classrooms in the school as well as to other programs.

Meetings. Viewing meetings as opportunities to collaborate takes some effort! Changing meetings to be more collaborative is really quite simple. It requires assuming that everyone at the meeting has something to offer and creating opportunities for everyone to contribute!

Taking charge of creating collaborations

Becoming a collaborator is well within the purview of each of us. It starts when we decide on a plan and take charge of the process of collaboration (Mitstifer, Wenberg, & Schatz, 1993). These authors encourage teachers to create collaborations — be the initiator rather than waiting for someone else to collaborate with you.

Try some of the following strategies to make collaboration work for you.

Offer to collaborate. A great way to get started collaborating is to share your strengths with others. Don't wait for a request — offer your help first.

Michael, a preschool teacher, is a creative genius. He is always able to see new ways to use materials, has many ideas about creative art activities, and does an excellent job of documenting children's work. During his tenure, he has become everyone's creative art and documentation collaborator. He freely offers ideas, advice, help on how to create documentations, and support for using materials creatively.

Identify potential collaborators. Start by identifying co-workers that you already trust and respect. Or pinpoint an excellent teacher from whom you would like to learn. Or, look within the normal channels of support in your school for someone who can help you become a better teacher.

Shien, a new teacher, has a child who is giving her fits. Unsure of what to do, she asked her coordinator if she could call for help if she needs it. Amy agreed and took the collaboration a step further. She would come into the classroom to help Shien and then provide a follow-up discussion each time she was called to share what she did, why she did it, and what might work next time. As a result, Shien's skills in handling a challenging child have grown (and the number of requests for help have diminished!).

Create time to talk, discuss, and reflect. Of all of the suggestions, this is the one most under the control of the teacher.

Cheryl has created a ritual that makes time for her to talk, discuss, and reflect with a variety of collaborators. She spends one or two lunch hours a month visiting other classrooms during nap time to talk with colleagues. One or two days a month, she observes other teachers in action in their classrooms, usually at the end of her day. And, once or twice a month, she sits with the director to reflect on her experiences with children in the classroom. None of these are scheduled, planned collaborations — they all occur when Cheryl is able to grab the time.

Joanne, on the other hand, has a teen-age son at home and wants to leave as soon as she can at the end of her shift. Her strategy for creating time to talk, discuss, and reflect is a more formal one. She requests that regular discussions and coaching be scheduled when time and resources allow. She makes these requests through the system her center uses for asking for time out of the classroom. Each request is specific — i.e., meet with Gwen to discuss room arrangement, meet with Kay to understand developmental assessments, etc.

Discover common ground. Most schools have their own locker rooms or teachers' lounges where teachers discuss issues, concerns, or problems. Collaborating teachers use these discussions to discover common ground and identify problems and concerns. Great collaboration comes from teachers deciding to reject the status quo and do something to address issues or solve problems.

Kathleen and Brooke discovered they both viewed the playground schedule as a big problem! The problem was that no one saw planning and preparing the outdoor environment as their responsibility — everyone thought someone else should do it. After discussing it between themselves, they decided to collaborate to propose a solution to the problem. They met together on their lunch breaks, asked experienced teachers what had worked in the past, pulled ideas out of the staff library, tossed around new ideas, and came up with a completely new way to plan and implement outdoor curriculum. They brought their ideas to a staff meeting, discussed them with their colleagues, and got agreement to try the new ideas out. Subsequent discussions among teachers refined ideas that didn't work and formalized the planning process. The latest collaboration among these two teachers is to conduct a mini training session at staff meeting to keep the improvements going and re-evaluate along the way to see if any modifications are needed.

Ask for support in collaborating. Some topics, problems, or situations require a different approach. Programs have different resources — some that teachers know about and some that they may not know about. Find out which resources are available in your school and collaborate with them.

Dr. Farley visits the school twice a month for collaboration meetings. Meetings are scheduled during nap time and teachers can request to attend if they feel that they have a need to get expert advise on children in their classrooms, parents who are challenging, or emotional curriculum ideas for implementation in the classroom. Dr. Farley helps teachers share observations and insights, and adds new observations and insights from a supporting discipline.

Ask for feedback. Most teachers want and need more feedback than they get (Albrecht, 1990). Great sources of feedback for teachers are co-teachers, parents, administrative staff, and others in the school. Collaborating to get feedback is a natural — particularly when it can be reciprocal. Ask a co-teacher to observe you and give you feedback about a specific area of your teaching and reciprocate by doing the same for her. Both will likely get good feelings about skills that are already in place as well as identifying new skills that could be practiced or learned.

Masami's native language is Japanese. Although his English skills are very good, he is always concerned about using English appropriately in speaking and writing, particularly when he is taking dictation from the children. He has perfected several strategies for making sure that his language models are good for the children. For example, he audio-tapes children's dictation so he can listen to the recording and make sure he represented what was said accurately. He has created several collaborative relationships. The school's director serves as an editor when Masami writes notes to parents, articles for the newsletter, or completes assessments. His co-teacher serves as a real-time reviewer of the dictation on children's work and notes to parents.

Try new challenges. When you see a problem, ask to be part of the solution. See if there is a role you can play in helping. If you don't have an idea about how to solve a problem, offer to discuss and review others' ideas. Plan a brain-storming session with a colleague to come up with possible solutions no one has ever considered.

Rene felt frustrated by the frequency of scheduling problems. She volunteered to work on the schedule with the idea she could help solve the problems she saw cropping up repeatedly. She was right. But, in the process, she discovered that her point of view in scheduling, though valuable, was classroom focused and lacked the broader view a manager might take. So she and her supervisor worked out an approach where each checked the other's work, insuring that the schedule met the classroom teachers' needs and the manager's needs as well.

These few examples highlight the range and potential of collaboration among teachers. Take the first steps to collaborate now — your teaching practice and your professional skills will improve in the process.

References

Albrecht, K. (1990). "Helping teachers grow: Strategies for diversifying performance evaluation and feedback." *Exchange*, *74*, 34-36.

Carter, M. (1998). "Principles and strategies for coaching and mentoring." *Exchange*, *120*, 82-86.

Gandini, L., Edwards, C., & Forman, G. (1998). *The hundred languages of children: The Reggio approach — advanced reflections.* Greenwich, CT: Ablex.

Gandini, L., Edwards, C., & Forman, G. (1993). *The hundred languages of children: The Reggio approach.* Greenwich, CT: Ablex.

Love, F. E., & Rowland, S. T. (1999). "The ABCs of mentoring beginning teachers." *Dimensions, 27*(4), 8-10.

Mitstifer, D. I., Wenberg, B. G., & Schatz, P. E. (1993). *Mentoring: The human touch.* East Lansing, MI: Kappa Omicron Nu, Inc.

Scanlon, P. N. (1988). "How to implement a coaching program in your center." *Exchange, 59,* 35-37.

Tertell, E. A., Klein, S. M., & Jewett, J. L. (1998). *When teachers reflect.* Washington, DC: NAEYC.

Kay Albrecht, Ph.D., is president of Innovations in Early Childhood Education, Houston, Texas, and the academic editor of *Exchange*. Teaching in some capacity has been the bulk of Kay's life work, beginning with her first assignment as a preschool teacher in a laboratory setting. She has continued her work with young children and the adults who teach them ever since. She has been the director of a nationally accredited early childhood program and on the faculty at four universities. Her consulting specialties include writing, management, and director and teacher professional development. A frequent contributor to *Exchange*, she is the author of "Out of the Box Early Childhood Training Kits," *The Right Fit: Recruiting, Selecting, and Orienting Staff*, published by New Horizons, and co-author, along with Linda Miller, of the *Innovations series of curriculum, development, and training materials for infants, toddlers, and preschoolers* published by Gryphon House.

COLLABORATION

Building Collaborations Between Programs and Within the Community

by Roberta Bergman

There is no question that the concept of collaboration among programs serving children and families has value. Collaborations among individual child care providers or between child care and the public schools, child care and Head Start, providers and child health organizations, providers and training institutions, and among funders have repeatedly fulfilled their potential to leverage scarce resources, eliminate unnecessary duplications, reach larger markets, and increase families' access to a wider range of services than they might otherwise use or even know about. Collaborations are encouraged across the country by public and private funding sources alike. It appears that plays well with others is a measure on which early childhood professionals are still graded.

The question attached to the concept of collaboration is how to make it work. Business collaborations occur all the time. They're known as strategic alliances, partnerships, joint ventures, cooperative agreements, consortia, or similar terms. Why and how they work provides some useful guidelines.

Lessons from the corporate world

Corporations collaborate when it will help them meet their own strategic objectives. There is something of measurable value in the collaboration for each partner . . . they're not collaborating to please someone else or just to be nice. Instead, they enter into a collaborative relationship in which they will share their resources with others in order for their own company to be able to do a better job — extend its reach, reduce inefficiencies, create a new product or service, acquire a new technology, earn new revenues, etc.

Case studies reveal that these collaborations work best among partners of equal strength who come together to complement each others' work. The partners may have unique products or services, serve different geographic areas, or offer distinctive functional strengths (finance, marketing, technology, for example). Collaborations are less likely to succeed if the partners overlap each others' products or services to a high degree or serve the same markets. Somebody will be asked to give up something they've worked hard to establish — not an easy way to launch a cooperative venture. If the partners are struggling to bridge the same gaps, collaborating is all but pointless. As one wag labeled the attempted recovery efforts of two ailing banks during that industry's turbulence in the 1980s, "It's the mortally wounded joining forces with the terminally ill."

When a weak organization collaborates with a substantially stronger partner in order to tap its strength or to gain new competencies, it is unlikely to be able to contribute sufficiently to the relationship, creating an imbalance which can result in failure. On the other hand, one partner may be seen as weaker than another — not because the organization is less competent but because it is smaller: has fewer facilities, fewer customers, fewer employees, less money. Collaborations involving partners with such perceived weaknesses work best when these partners assume responsibility for a vital function within the collaboration, thus assuring them equal stature.

Corporations collaborate around a specific purpose. Hotel chains, for example, have formed collaborations in which they share marketing and reservations systems. Airlines collaborate with each other to route passengers to destinations they don't serve themselves. A company with a specific technology may collaborate with another which has needed distribution channels. These companies don't give up their identities; they don't change their missions or their corporate cultures; they simply decide it is in their best interests to work together in a specific way.

Creating proactive collaborations in your own community

Although many business collaborations have developed over the years when two or more companies decided that they each had resources that, combined, could meet a new market need, most collaborations in the early childhood field have occurred in response to decreased dollars or increased competition. Relatively few have originated as the result of entrepreneurial urges or strategic planning processes. Yet that's where most of the potential lies.

So in thinking about collaborations within your community, look first at your own strategic plan. What resources do you need to achieve your objectives that you don't have now? Who else has them? What could you bring to the table that is of value to the other parties? What would a collaboration achieve that the individual members could not accomplish on their own?

Again, most people would agree that collaboration is positive — it's nice to cooperate, to include others, to share, to extend a helping hand. But be careful not to confuse the virtues of collaboration with the reasons for doing it — reasons which must be clear and justifiable for each party. Collaborations require considerable effort if they are to succeed, so they must be perceived by the participants as being worth the work. What's in it for me (my organization)? — as crass as that may sound — has to be asked and answered. And while added and/or better services for children and their families should be the ultimate goal, the answer needs to be more immediate and measurable.

There are many ways to improve or expand services. Collaboration is often a good approach, but it's only one approach. Is it the right one for your organization?

In considering potential partners, think about the following:

■ Which partner(s) will control access to the families who will be served?

■ Who will determine eligibility, enroll families, represent the collaboration to the parents?

■ What will the key positions be in the collaboration? Which partner(s) will staff more of these positions?

■ What financial contribution will be required of each partner? Which partner is more able and willing to invest its funds?

■ For which partner(s) is the collaboration truly strategic?

These are important considerations because they determine the value of each partner's bargaining chips. Even if each partner makes what is perceived as an equal contribution at the beginning of the collaboration, the balance of power may shift over time. One partner's funding could decrease, another's customer base could change, key players could move on, and so forth. The challenge for the collaboration is to decide whether to try to keep strengths and contributions always in balance or to accept that shifts in the balance of power are inevitable and plan accordingly.

Principles of successful collaborations

What makes collaborations within the community work?

1. The partners should commit to the collaboration for a set period of time. Five years is a good target as collaborations need time to mature. And they take time. Successful collaborations are high maintenance: more meetings, more minutes, more action items, more phone calls. Each partner must agree to spend the requisite hours.

2. Mutual trust is required not only between the partnering organizations but also between the individuals involved in the collaboration. The growth of this trust is the reason the collaboration needs time. Although the partnering organizations may already respect each other through direct experience or by reputation, all the people who do the work of the collaboration may not know each other when they first come together. They require time to build the relationships that are essential to achieving the collaboration's purposes.

3. Collaborations are most likely to succeed when the partners are like-minded and have a shared strategy or similar goals. There is agreement not only on what the collaboration is to accomplish but also how it will do it. Further, there are mutually accepted performance criteria or standards of quality. Everyone understands by what measures the collaboration's work will be evaluated.

4. The partners agree to share resources, strengths, and information. There are connections between the partners at key points in each organization. The financial people in each organization talk with each other; the information systems people communicate; the program people meet regularly. What one partner knows that might affect the collaboration's work, all know. In addition, the people who represent their organizations within the collaboration are authorized to act on behalf of their organizations, or, if other decision-makers must be consulted, have quick access to these individuals.

5. The distinctive qualities brought by each partner (specialized expertise, access to specific markets, unique services) are what add value to the collaboration, not the size of the partner's budget, clientele, or workforce. As a result, each partner has an

Resources

The most visible collaborations across the country have been established between Head Start and child care programs in an effort to expand and improve services for low-income families. The Federal Child Care and Head Start Bureaus have themselves partnered in a new initiative called Quality in Linking Together: Early Education Partnerships (the QUILT), designed to support and foster early education partnerships on the local level.

Among the QUILT's services are: collecting, developing, and disseminating descriptive information on partnership structures and collaborative strategies; developing training materials and publications providing guidance and fiscal strategies to promote partnerships among early education programs; delivering on-site technical assistance for Head Start, child care, prekindergarten, and other early education providers; and conducting national and regional training, forums, and meetings for early education staffs that encourage and advance partnering. The QUILT can be accessed through its toll-free hotline — (877) to-QUILT (867-8458) — or at its web site (www.QUILT.org).

Children's Defense Fund (CDF) has published a book which includes glimpses of more than 20 collaborations across the country and samples of documents used by these programs (assessment tools, collaboration contracts, staffing charts, budgets, etc.). *Working Together for Children: Head Start and Child Care Partnerships*, by Nicole Oxendine Poersch and Helen Blank, is available from CDF at 25 E Street NW, Washington, DC 20001, (202) 628-8787, or through its web site www.childrensdefense.org.

Your local child care resource and referral agency (CCR&R) may be another resource. Many CCR&Rs across the country are helping build partnerships in their communities. Because they tend to have a big-picture perspective along with good local information on child care supply and demand, they are often able to bring community partners together to fashion innovative solutions to systemic problems. Information on how to contact the child care resource and referral agency in your community can be obtained from the National Association of Child Care Resource and Referral Agencies (NACCRRA) at 1319 F Street NW, Suite 810, Washington, DC 20004, (202) 393-5501, or through its web site (www.NACCRRA.org).

Finally, there are a variety of books on strategic alliances, written for business audiences but with principles that clearly apply to collaborations in child care. *Alliance Advantage: The Art of Creating Value Through Partnering*, by Yves L. Doz and Gary Hamel (published by Harvard Business School Press), is labeled by one reviewer as "a must-read book for anyone involved in or contemplating a strategic alliance." *The Power of Two: How Companies of All Sizes Can Build Alliance Networks That Generate Business Opportunities*, by John K. Conlon and Melissa Giovagnoli (Jossey-Bass Publishers), emphasizes the personal aspects of alliances which must focus on relationships rather than transactions. These kinds of resources can be useful; check with your local librarian, your Internet or community book store, or the faculty of a nearby university business school for recommended reading.

equal voice in the collaboration. There are as many reasons to collaborate as there are ways to do so. The key is in the value added by each partner — what each partner brings that another needs. When their strengths are combined, the collaboration becomes greater than the sum of its parts.

Roberta Bergman has over 30 years' experience in the development, management, and marketing of child care and early education programs, including the design and implementation of several successful collaborations. She is currently Director of Funding at Voyager Expanded Learning®, a leading provider of in-school core reading programs, reading and math intervention programs, and professional development programs for school districts throughout the United States.

Child Care in
Unique Environments

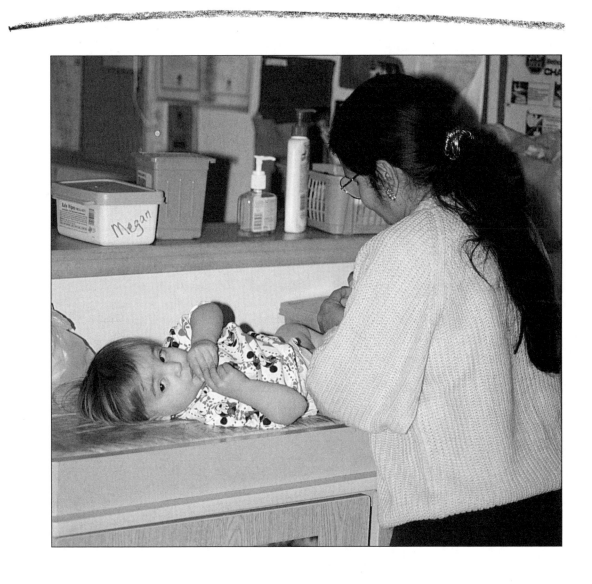

CHILD CARE IN UNIQUE ENVIRONMENTS

Strengthening Families in Special Environments

by Wayna Buch

With the increase of drug use, more young children in our programs are coping with parental incarceration. Teachers say they see an increase of challenging behaviors and low motivation towards learning due to parental loss. Young children grieving their losses struggle in social groups, often acting out their anger and frustration upon peers or caregivers. Their sense of well being is shattered, as is their sense of self worth. If both parents face incarceration, the loss increases. Often children must live with aging grandparents, relatives, or foster families.

The statistics are compelling: **60 percent of children with imprisoned parents are younger than eight.** Children of prisoners are six times more likely to be incarcerated at some point in their lives. There is growing recognition, locally and nationally, of the need to foster positive and more frequent communication between incarcerated parents and their children to strengthen families and break the cycle of incarceration.

The Urban Institute in Washington, DC reported that children, feeling the void of an imprisoned parent or family member, often succumb to developmental problems (2003). By age 2, children who have been left behind as infants become completely dependent on substitute caregivers and rarely ever bond with their parent. By age 6, that child may become more independent, but display socio-emotional impairment, traumatic stress reactions, and "survivor guilt." Between ages 7 and 10, a child shows less ability to overcome future emotional trauma.

Addressing an unmet need

Good Beginnings Alliance (GBA) is the intermediary organization dedicated to ensuring that in Hawaii there are programs in place to provide parents with the knowledge, skills, and capacity to provide their young children with safe and nurturing environments. In response to a need for the children of incarcerated parents, GBA developed a partnership with Waiawa Correctional Facility and two local organizations — The Coalition for Dads and The Institute For Family Enrichment (TIFFE, Nurturing Fathers Program). The partnership resulted in the creation of the SKIP (Supporting Keiki of Incarcerated Parents) Project.

Supporting Keiki of Incarcerated Parents (SKIP) Project is a community-based family strengthening project aimed at secondary prevention of child abuse and neglect among children of incarcerated parents. SKIP is designed to increase incarcerated and custodial parents' ability to provide safe and nurturing environments for their young children while incarcerated. The SKIP model works with incarcerated fathers at Waiawa Correctional Facility, due to be released and reunited with their children within 6 months to one year, and their families.

SKIP goals are to reconnect parent and child prior to release and to strengthen family bonds. The interactive, hands-on learning and guidance of parenting skills allows the parent and children to learn and play together in a safe, facilitated, and structured learning environment, also known as a playgroup.

Early childhood program in a special environment

Playgroups, or parent participation programs, as some call them, take place throughout the state of Hawaii. These

Note: Incarceration of a parent affects all children regardless of age.
However, for the sake of this article, the focus is on young children coping with the impact of parental incarceration.

programs take place in communities and are seen as an informal continuum of care for families unable to access preschool. There are many different models of playgroups; some, like SKIP, occur in special environments or are specific to an identified need, such as the playgroup for children with special needs. All programs have common outcomes and components:

- parent-child interactive activities
- literacy and language development
- information, resources, and family supports
- culturally relevant and developmentally appropriate curriculum and environment
- parent education and leadership training

In spring 2003, the SKIP Project initiated a 13-week pilot project, the first of its kind in Hawaii. The concept of children going into prison presented some challenges and opposition, but also more support than anticipated. Seizing the opportunity to provide needed services to a gap group, we forged ahead by conducting a playgroup at the Waiawa Correctional Facility for inmate fathers simultaneously enrolled in a therapeutic curriculum called Nurturing Fathers. For most of the inmates, the Good Beginnings Playgroup was the first opportunity they had in years to spend quality time with their children on a regular basis. While the Nurturing Fathers classes allow fathers the chance to reflect and learn about their childhood parental role models, the playgroup offers them the opportunity to practice parenting skills, with a coach.

Fathers in training

Fathers who apply go through an application and interview process. Once accepted they receive hands-on early childhood training using the Good Beginnings Alliance curriculum "Supporting Parents as First Teachers" (SPAFT), for five weeks prior to the start of the playgroup. SPAFT prepares them for caregiving responsibilities. During their SPAFT classes, fathers learn the importance of the early years and their role as First Teachers to children. For some, this concept is very new and terrifying. The adult learner curriculum teaches fathers about child development, setting up the environment, appropriate ways to communicate with children and, how children play and learn. Fathers all learn and practice how to change diapers, set a snack table, do finger plays, sing songs, and guide children through routines and transitions. By the end of the five weeks, fathers are able to transform an adult education classroom into a safe learning environment in preparation for the children to arrive at playgroup.

SKIP play and learn mornings

Before morning activities begin, the fathers gather for "Talk Story" to check in, discuss the day's parent-child activity, and

get guidance tips. Once the children arrive at the door, fathers are on! Under the guidance of a trained early childhood teacher and assistant, fathers practice skills and knowledge learned in their classes. In this safe, supportive environment, they learn to accept and become comfortable with their role and responsibilities as "Dad." It is important to note that SKIP is not a "visit" — it is a time to work through newly learned skills and knowledge. The primary focus is on parental guidance and re-bonding of the parent and child relationship.

The value of the program is stated by Warden Ted Sakai who says, "This program has changed the way the men do time. It has made a positive difference on how the whole prison does business."

Further evidence of this fact comes from the fathers. One father shared how he was never a dad to his children and now hoped to have a "second chance." Three weeks later he sat comfortably on a cushion in the library area reading the *Kissing Hand* to his three children, ages 6, 8, and 10. As he read he kissed each child's hand. His son giggled in delight pointed to him, then said, "I love you, Daddy."

Later, during closing "Talk Story," this dad shared how he felt "blessed" because he was given a gift he thought was lost forever — the love of his children who thought of him as "uncle."

Testimonial evidence that it works!

Media has filmed and written much about SKIP over the years. A six-year-old child, who wanted to be interviewed, shared with a reporter how much the SKIP playgroup meant to her. She shared, "I get to be with my daddy and do things with him. I get to see him and know he is fine."

Another father shared that he and his daughter had "no relationship." He said he saw her five times in five years. By her third playgroup he watched her as she sat playing intently with sand and water toys. Dad seemed mesmerized by her playfulness. She turned to him and said, "Daddy, I am making you and me a castle to live in and play in by the beach. It is a sand castle." She reached for his hand and invited him to sit with her as she completed the structure. Tears welled up in dad's eyes. Later at "Talk Story" he shared, "She called me daddy and wanted me near her. I can never return to this place; my daughter needs me, she needs her Dad!"

When parents get that they are important to their children, they begin to make attitude and life changes. Whether or not they return home, they seem to understand for the first time, that THEY are essential to the well-being of their child, and being in prison is very hard for children. A father told a reporter, "I get it now! When I do time, my whole family does time, right along with me."

Nurturing the caregiver

SKIP also nurtures the caregiver, parent, grandparent, or foster parent who brings the children to the facility. They do not enter the playgroup room; instead, they meet in an adjoining room with a trained facilitator. After check-in they discuss common issues, learn about child development, get information on resources, or just enjoy down time. A caregiver shared, "It is the only time in a week that I have to myself. It gives me time to just be with adults and take care of me."

Another mom shared how she works at night, sleeps during the day for a couple of hours, then "takes care of life," until it is time for her to pick up her children. After tending to their needs, she kisses them good night, then studies until it is time to leave for work. Her parents care for the children at night. The playgroup is so important that she makes the extra effort to be there each week. She says, "It is my time to breathe and regroup."

Beyond the walls

The SKIP project has been such a success that Good Beginnings is receiving requests from other correctional facilities and social service agencies to be trained in providing SKIP services. SKIP could not happen without partners committed to strengthening families and to decreasing the cycle of child abuse and neglect. Each partner brings to the program resources and funds to support families with little or no help raising children who are struggling with parental incarceration. Partners also help identify needed teacher and community training to increase awareness of parental incarceration.

Most remarkably, some parents exiting prison have joined us in our efforts to expand services to families and children by advocating for more such programs in male, female, and youth facilities. They share their stories, help with evaluating and reviewing the program, and offer advice to guide our work. They have become natural partners.

Challenges and barriers

SKIP is not without its share of challenges and barriers. However, because of the committed partners, funders, and the correctional facility, we work to negotiate and address each challenge head on. As Warden Sakai stated, "In the end, it really is about all of us doing what is best for our kids!"

References

The Urban Institute. (November, 2003). "Families Left Behind: The Hidden Costs of Incarceration and Re-entry" Report.

Wayna is an Early Childhood Trainer and Community Program Manager with Good Beginnings Alliance in Hawaii. Wayna developed and coordinates an innovative program called, Supporting Keiki (Children) of Incarcerated Parents-SKIP held at Waiawa Correctional Facility. SKIP is a collaborative partnership early childhood program that strengthens families and supports children coping with parental incarceration. Wayna also facilitates training classes using a curriculum she helped to develop called, Supporting Parents as First Teachers (SPAFT). Wayna's passion for working with young children came from being orphaned at an early age, living in nine foster homes in nine years, and later becoming a foster parent. She has extensive experiences in working with children and families at risk, those with special needs, and families impacted by substance abuse and/or incarceration.

Using Beginnings Workshop to Train Teachers by Kay Albrecht

Lessons Learned: Validating families as first educators of their children is important work. Explore ways to support parents in your program as first teachers of their children using this article as a springboard.

Me, too!: Do families enrolled in your program need support in interacting successfully with their children? Consider implementing a SKIP-like program with families. Use this article as a starting place, then make the ultimate program your own.

Leveraging the Model: Explore connecting with a local correctional institution to replicate this interesting model.

CHILD CARE IN UNIQUE ENVIRONMENTS

Reaching the Most Vulnerable Children

by Elizabeth Ruethling

In recent years, advocates and policy makers from around the world have made tremendous gains in the international community's commitment to extending basic education to all children. From the *Education for All* objectives set forth in Jomtien, Thailand, in 1990 to the more recent pledges of the *Millennium Development Goals*, the conviction that universal education is not only a human right but also an achievable aspiration has earned widespread support.

From the very outset of this movement, the importance of early childhood care and development (ECCD) has been clearly referenced. Indeed, formally adopted by the World Education Forum held in Dakar, Senegal, in 2000, the collective commitments affirm the international goal of "expanding and improving comprehensive early childhood care and education, especially for the most vulnerable and disadvantaged children" (UNESCO, 2005). While experts are not always in agreement regarding the precise outcomes of ECCD in developing countries, research shows that young children who participate in such programs are more likely to succeed in primary school and to remain enrolled through grades higher than do their peers who did not attend preschool (World Bank, 2004).

Beyond increasing primary school enrollment and retention, however, many communities around the world have come to view the care of young children as a crucial component of broader social change. Not only do ECCD activities improve the academic and developmental potentials of young children, but they also offer employment to local individuals; provide a respite from the harsh daily realities of children of impoverished families; and enable mothers and older siblings to work and attend school, respectively, by freeing them from their child care duties. By providing children with a safe environment, opportunities for experiential learning, and some basic social skills, community-run ECCD programs can play an important role in helping to break cycles of discrimination, exploitation, and disempowerment.

The Global Fund for Children (GFC) is a non-profit grant maker endeavoring to support small, grassroots organizations working to improve the lives of vulnerable children globally. To this end, GFC has helped to fund a number of community-based organizations that run preschools, child care facilities, and other programs for young children living in some of the poorest places in the world. In most cases, these programs were not designed or implemented by ECCD experts, nor were they initiated as a response to the growing international focus on improving ECCD as a means to increase academic success. Rather, these programs evolved as pointed answers to the real problems facing communities, each with its own unique methods and set of desired outcomes. Such organizations have limited financial means; more than half of GFC's grantee partners operate on budgets of less than $100,000 per year. GFC's responsive and institutionally focused grant-making approach ensures that these grantee partners can maintain the entrepreneurial and creative spirit that makes their programs most effective.

The three brief overviews below are intended to demonstrate ways in which ECCD programs have been implemented as a means to improve both the immediate conditions as well as the long-term opportunities of disadvantaged children. From providing the children of prostitutes protection from the hazards of the red-light district during the nighttime, to helping to prevent young children's exposure to dangerous work in garbage dumps, to offering the only kindergarten in a rural town in Africa, these programs provide practical solutions to complex social problems.

Prerana: Night Care Center for the Children of Prostitutes Mumbai, India

Due to extreme poverty and a lack of opportunities, many women turn to commercial sex work as one of the few avenues available to them that will provide an income to support themselves and their families. While the lives of these women are dangerous and abusive, it is their children who often suffer even more. At night, when the women are working as prostitutes, many children have no one to care for them; their mothers are forced either to leave them unattended in the slums, where they are vulnerable to crime and other dangers, or to take their children along while they work, introducing them at a young age to the realities of violence, exploitation, and prejudice. More than any other sector of society, these children are likely to become sex workers themselves. Having been exposed to the world of sexual exploitation, young girls and boys are easily lured into the commercial sex trade, thus continuing the cycle of abuse and poverty.

Based in Kamathipura, Mumbai's largest red-light district, Prerana (which means "inspiration") has worked since 1986 to protect the human rights of sexually exploited women and their children. Established in 1990, Prerana's Night Care Center for children of prostitutes was one of the first of its kind anywhere in the world. Mothers who hope to spare their children the harmful realities of the red-light district and to discourage them from becoming second-generation prostitutes entrust them to the Night Care Center. Here, children aged two to six are provided with nourishment, baths, recreation, and a safe place to sleep. The center is open from 5:30 p.m. to 9:30 a.m., thus keeping young children away from the streets during the red-light district's busiest time. The model of the Night Care Center has been replicated throughout the world as an effective means of diminishing psychological, emotional, and physical harm afflicted on youth living in red-light districts. In 2001, GFC became the first U.S.-based funder of Prerana. Since that time, GFC has not only provided $44,500 in direct funding, it has also leveraged new funders for Prerana; helped to bring Priti Patkar, Prerana's founder and director, to the 2003 Global Philanthropy Forum to present her work; and supported Prerana's efforts in strategic organizational development.

Once children have become accustomed to participating in activities at the Night Care Center, the majority of them remain enrolled in ongoing Prerana programs, receiving educational support, health care, and other services throughout their adolescence. After nearly 20 years of serving its community, Prerana continues to find new ways to assist and empower their young and growing charges, from the purchasing of necessary school supplies to arranging for their enrollment in boarding schools. However, despite the organization's ongoing programmatic growth and the expansion of its advocacy work, one of the most effective methods of increasing community mobilization and support continues to be the Night Care Center and other services for young children. By attracting the early participation of both mothers and children, Prerana can begin to introduce them to additional services geared toward preventing second-generation prostitution and other further exploitation of this highly at-risk population of young people.

Asociación Promoción y Desarrollo de la Mujer Nicaragüense — ACAHUALT: Community Preschool for Families Working in Garbage Dumps Managua, Nicaragua

The community of Acahualinca is one of the poorest in the city of Managua. Approximately 16,000 inhabitants live in crowded, substandard housing without benefit of basic public services such as potable water, sewage systems, or access to medical care. This community is adjacent to the municipal dump, where garbage is deposited every day. With only 10 percent of Acahualinca's residents formally employed, many residents make their living from scavenging through the garbage for recyclable materials or items to sell. A 2001 survey found that only 22 percent of Acahualinca's families were earning the median income needed to purchase household goods for one month, and one fifth lived on less than a dollar a day. In addition, only 29 percent of the population has completed primary school, and only half of those who enter secondary school remain enrolled until graduation.

The Asociación Promoción y Desarrollo de la Mujer Nicaragüense — ACAHUALT (meaning "Association for the Promotion and Development of Nicaraguan Women") is a community leader in combating discrimination and violence against women and girls. In 2001, ACAHUALT started a community preschool program for very poor families that are unable to afford an education for their children. Many of these children's parents are unemployed and so, in order to survive, both the children and the adults scavenge in the garbage dump for items to sell. The preschool has three classes for children aged three to six, divided by age group, and each class serves approximately 25 students. The program runs five days a week from 8:30 to 11:00 a.m. and uses a curriculum and teaching methodology approved by the Ministry of Education. By using these materials, the preschool is certified by the state, and the children are thus able to move into the formal school system upon graduation from the preschool. By improving their students' chances of succeeding in primary school, the community preschool is also helping to combat initial exposure to hazardous child labor, ensuring that — at least for a few hours each day — children remain in the classroom and out of the garbage dumps.

The preschool and related services have proved enormously popular, and with support from GFC beginning in 2004, ACAHUALT has increased attendance at its preschool and is now able to offer specialized attention to children who need psychological care, family counseling, or legal assistance. Trainings are provided to parents and to teachers on topics such as human rights and gender and domestic violence. Underscoring the organization's holistic approach to the well-being of the community's children, each child and his or her family receive health services such as screenings for parasites, malnutrition, and communicable diseases. By addressing the needs of working families in a comprehensive, flexible manner, ACAHUALT's community preschool and other services create real improvements in the lives of its beneficiaries.

Jifunze Project:
Early Learning Center for Rural Children
Kibaya, Tanzania

Kibaya, with approximately 20,000 residents, is the largest town in northern Tanzania's isolated Kiteto District. Located in the southern point of the Masai homeland, Kiteto District is one of the most impoverished districts in the country due to its remote location, a shortage of clean water, and a very limited supply of electricity. Home to a diverse mixture of different tribes, Kibaya lacks even a single kindergarten classroom for its over 3,000 preschool-age children. Instead, these children must gather with their teachers beneath trees, in dining halls, church sanctuaries, and teachers' personal homes, crouching in the dirt and outlining their lessons in the sand. Given the extreme shortage of resources, most kindergarten classes average around 100 students. Because of the large classes, learning takes place predominantly by memorization of sounds and syllables. This lack of a solid preschool education makes the transition to primary school extremely challenging, especially for children living in rural areas where village culture is often very different from school culture. Less than 50 percent of school-age children in Kiteto District are able to successfully complete their primary-school education.

Launched in 1999, the Jifunze (meaning "learning") Project's Community Education Resource Center aims to remedy the problems of education for Kiteto District's children by working alongside community members to help them create innovative, empowering, and sustainable educational opportunities that will expand their possibilities for livelihood and enrich their lives. As a program of this community center, the Early Learning Center (ELC) was launched in 2002 specifically to address the lack of kindergarten resources. The ELC enables children aged four to six to develop the skills and confidence necessary for

successful performance and retention in primary school, while also building the capacity of local early-education teachers. In addition, the ELC exposes children to a wide variety of educational toys and materials, stimulating their curiosity and appetite for learning. With general support grants from GFC totaling $25,000 over three years, Jifunze has been able to provide English language classes at the ELC, produce its own books, and offer AIDS-awareness programs, in addition to supporting the core activities of the organization.

The ELC was established and is now coordinated by Christina Gabriel, who, after conducting site visits to and research of various kindergartens around Tanzania, designed the center using a combination of indigenous, Montessori, and other early education philosophies. She is currently the most experienced early childhood education teacher in the Kibaya area; and the ELC serves as not only a local kindergarten, but also as a nationally recognized model for ECCD. While the ELC helps to build a strong foundation for the educational aspirations of this neglected population, it is but the first step in a range of academic and self-improvement services for life-long learning.

These are but three examples of the creative, relevant, and dynamic ECCD programs being implemented by community-based groups throughout the world. As with all of GFC's grantee partners, these organizations have identified realistic, responsive approaches for improving the lives of underserved children and ensuring for them a more promising future.

References

UNESCO. (August 12, 2005). "Education for All: Dakar Framework for Action."
www.unesco.org/education/efa/ed_for_all/dakfram_eng.shtml

World Bank. (June 2004). "Education Notes: Getting an Early Start on Early Child Development."
http://siteresources.worldbank.org/EDUCATION/Resources/Education-Notes/EdNotes_ECD_2.pdf

Elizabeth Ruethling is Global Fund for Children's senior program officer for Asia and Eastern Europe. Elizabeth became involved with the work of GFC as an intern during the spring and summer of 2000, assisting the executive director in writing grant proposals and researching content for future Shakti for Children books. In the winter of 2001 she volunteered for the long-time GFC grantee partner Ruchika Social Service Organisation in Bhubaneswar, India, where she helped to develop promotional materials and to draft grant proposals. Elizabeth graduated from Northwestern University with bachelor degrees in Asian Studies and International Studies.

Using Beginnings Workshop to Train Teachers by Kay Albrecht

Join the Global ECE Community: Add copies of the referenced declarations to you professional development library so your teachers understand these goals.

Explore the Wide, Wide World: Check out the listed web sites for more insight into the wide world of ECE.

CHILD CARE IN UNIQUE ENVIRONMENTS

Working With Homeless Young Children and Families

by Karin Elliott and Sarah Fujiwara

With the number of young homeless children and families in the United States increasing at a rapid rate, homeless families are the largest and fastest growing part of the homeless population. Approximately 1.35 million children experience homelessness each year in the United States, with more than half under the age of six. The majority of these families are headed by single mothers (The Better Homes Fund, 1999).

Thirty years ago child and family homelessness did not exist to the degree it does today. Two of the most significant reasons for the increase are the lack of affordable housing in our country coupled with poverty. Many families become homeless because they earn low wages and cannot keep up with expenses. Many families also lack a network or support system on which they can rely in a crisis. Families also become homeless as a result of domestic violence, physical and mental health issues, and substance abuse.

Many families who become homeless live doubled-up with friends or relatives before they move into shelters. Families often live in campgrounds, in cars, and in other situations that are unsafe for children. Often they move from one living situation to the next, exposing children to many transitions. Children experience the loss of homes, neighborhoods, relatives, friends, pets, and even favorite toys. Beyond the many material losses, these vulnerable children lose the feelings of safety, security, and stability in their lives.

How families struggle

Tasha is a single mother struggling to raise two young children, two and four years old. Tasha barely managed to pay rent for an apartment and cover expenses on her salary as an administrative assistant at a health care company. While she was fortunate to have her children enrolled in pa state subsidized child care center, paying even the small parent fees was a challenge. She

fell behind in payments and eventually the center had to terminate her child care because of non-payment. Tasha was told she could not access state funded child care until she repaid what she owed the center, but she was unable to do this.

Tasha's situation spiraled out of control. She had no one to care for her children and missed several days of work. Missed days led to job loss. Unable to pay her rent, Tasha and her children lost their apartment. Tasha applied for state funded emergency family shelter, and has been in a shelter in Boston for nine months. She is hopeful that she will be able to access child care, find a job, and find permanent housing.

There are different types of shelters for families. Shelter systems vary from state to state. A family may apply to a public welfare state department for emergency shelter in some states or there may be a decentralized system where families may contact many shelters looking for space. Shelter types include:

- **congregate family shelters:** each family has one bedroom

- **domestic violence shelters:** located in confidential locations

- **scattered site shelters:** often apartments rented by the sheltering agency for larger families

- **teen shelters:** provide specific services for pregnant and parenting teenagers

- **substance abuse and treatment shelters:** provide support for families with addiction

Shelters play an important role in providing a safe place for families to stay until they can find permanent housing. However, there are challenges to shelter life. Families have little privacy, must raise their children in a public setting, and adhere to many shelter rules. Shelter stays are becoming longer, growing from three to six months to over a year. Many families have nowhere else to go and experience stress that has a significant impact on family functioning, children's development, and sadly, the hope for a successful future.

What the research tells us

Research studies have shown that children experiencing homelessness face many challenges, including increased health problems, developmental delays, mental health challenges, increased anxiety and depression, behavioral problems, and lower educational achievement (The Better Homes Fund, 1999). Delays in motor, sensory, language/cognition, and social-emotional development are common. Homelessness also impacts the parent, most frequently the mother. Over one-third of homeless mothers have a chronic health problem, and almost 40 percent have been hospitalized for medical treatment (National Coalition for the Homeless, June 1999). Accessing health care, including mental health care is often difficult for homeless families. Many homeless families do not have routine health care, but rather use emergency rooms as their primary source of health care, which contributes to children's health problems.

Thanks to a recent emphasis on the importance of the early years and scientific brain research, the connection between early experiences, brain development, and later success in life has been proven. When young children are exposed to repeated stress, such as continued homelessness, this can negatively impact early brain development. Positive interactions and environments, as well as early interventions that promote positive social-emotional development, help children *bounce back*, and experience a solid foundation for positive growth and development (National Resource Council and Institute of Medicine, 2000).

We know that quality, comprehensive early care and education helps support children's development. Horizons for Homeless Children (HHC), a non-profit agency in Massachusetts, operates two child care centers which provide a nurturing environment for the children, while offering families support and services to help them achieve economic self-sufficiency.

The National Center on Family Homelessness (NCFH) recently conducted an evaluation of Horizons for Homeless Children's Community Centers (CCC) to determine the impact of the HHC child care on children and mothers in the program. A control group consisting of families living in area shelters not served by CCCs was followed; some of the children attended other child care programs and others did not. The evaluation looked at the impact of HHC child care on the homeless children and parents who received specialized parent support and assistance as they transitioned into permanent housing compared to those not in the HHC program. The study took place over five years and included 100 families at baseline, 47 of whom were CCC families. The number of families at the evaluation follow-up was 54, with 25 from the CCC.

Statistically significant findings indicated that the children who were enrolled in the CCC showed greater improvement in their vocabulary, receptive language skills, and early academic skills when compared to children in a comparison group. When asked about their perceptions of the CCC impact on their children, the majority of mothers indicated that the CCC helped their child be more confident, and ready for school, and helped identify and work on areas of need. The CCC mothers in the study indicated that they experienced higher levels of self-esteem at follow-up, were more focused on financial independence, felt more motivated to be self sufficient, were more likely to be working on a GED or other form of education, had developed a support network, and were more likely to be employed than those in the comparison group. In addition, CCC families experienced a higher degree of housing stability and were more likely to obtain subsidized housing.

Turning research into strategies: What can we do?

In order to use research findings that demonstrate the importance of positive early learning experiences, we need to turn this information into everyday knowledge and practice. Certain strategies are helpful when thinking about creating positive experiences for homeless children, particularly in the child care setting.

At HHC teachers work on creating *supportive environments* for children. The emphasis is on creating a setting that promotes stability, consistency, structure, and safety. Many homeless children have not had these elements in their lives; and by providing these, the stressful situation of experiencing homelessness can be somewhat alleviated. Examples of ways in which to achieve a supportive environment are to create a calm setting with classroom colors, artwork, and activities. Thinking about how the classroom is organized can help, as will placing a reading/quiet time corner out of the way of the classroom entrance or the dramatic play area. Structure and routine are important to consider. The experience of predictable routines and activities will help children feel that they are more in control of their surroundings. Something as simple as involving children in decisions about new pictures on the walls or rearranging classroom items will help them feel involved and supported. Many homeless children have had unsafe experiences; anything that you can do to assure them that you are the *adult* and will keep them safe in the classroom setting is important.

As the result of a shelter referral, Tasha was able to enroll her children in the Community Children's Center at HHC. Now that her children are in care, she found a new job and is working towards permanent housing.

HHC touches the lives of over 1,500 homeless children each week by providing early education at its two child care centers, and through its Playspace Programs, which provide children in shelters with safe, supportive, and educational places to play. The Playspaces are staffed by volunteers, known as PALs (Playspace Activity Leaders) who commit to two hours a week for a minimum of six months. This program has expanded statewide in Massachusetts. Currently 800 PALs are active each week in family shelters across Massachusetts. HHC is also dedicated to sharing its knowledge about child and family homelessness through training, advocacy, policy change, and through partnering with other organizations to help solve the problem.

Take action!

HHC took action in the spring of 2005 by holding the Young Children Without Homes National Conference in Boston, Massachusetts. The conference brought together 550 participants from over 40 states to focus on the importance of quality early care and education in the lives of young homeless children birth to six. Integral to the conference was the message that scientific research shows how trauma, including homelessness, can impact a child's development. This message must be shared with providers, policymakers, and legislators in order to improve outcomes for young homeless children.

All of us can take action towards alleviating impacts of and ending child and family homelessness. Those in direct service can provide positive classroom experiences and promote supportive environments. We can all share information about child and family homelessness with providers, legislators, policymakers, administrators, and others working with children and families.

Strategies

- **Raise awareness:** Share information about child and family homelessness. As the problem grows, so must our ability to communicate with others about the facts, statistics, and impacts. Preparing brief fact sheets is one way to share information.

- **Improve access to quality child care and other services:** Collaborate with other providers on ways to help young homeless children and families access services such as child care, Head Start, Early Intervention, and more. Sharing information about available resources through referrals and networking is a good idea.

- **Partner:** Join in with other programs to make the best use of resources and provide important services. We can't all know everything about resources, but we can be prepared to hand out brochures from other programs or share contact numbers.

- **Talk to your legislators:** staying in touch with your legislators and staying on top of how legislation and policies impact homeless families is key. Make sure that your elected official has visited your program to understand firsthand how homelessness impacts children's lives. Making regular calls and visits to your legislators will let them know that you are an interested and educated constituent. Scheduling events, such as child care lobby days or legislative breakfasts makes the point even stronger: you and your agency will advocate for children and families who are homeless.

References

The Better Homes Fund. (1999). *Homeless Children: America's New Outcasts*. Newton, MA: The Better Homes Fund.

National Coalition for the Homeless. (June 1999). Fact Sheet #7.

National Resource Council and Institute of Medicine (2000). *From Neurons to Neighborhoods: The Science of Early Childhood Development*. Committee on Integrating the Science of Early Childhood Development. Jack P. Shonkoff and Deborah A. Phillips (eds.). Board on Children, Youth and Families, Commission on Behavioral and Social Sciences and Education. Washington, DC: National Academy Press.

Karin Elliott is the former Director of Training and Technical Assistance for Horizons for Homeless Children. She is knowledgeable in both early care and education and child development, as well as in working with children at risk.

Sarah Fujiwara is the Chief Programs Officer for Horizons for Homeless Children. She oversees the Training and Technical Assistance Program, the Playspace Programs, and the Community Children's Centers.

Using Beginnings Workshop to Train Teachers by Kay Albrecht

Making a Difference: Elliott proposes that taking action about homelessness is every early childhood educator's responsibility. Explore strategies for taking action with teachers and families. Identify ways that make sense for your program and pursue them.

Thinking About Homelessness with Children: Ann Pelo's article "Supporting Young Children as Activists — Anti-bias Project Work" (Exchange, March/April 2002) poses ways to explore difficult topics such as homelessness when children ask questions or show interest in such topics. Copy this terrific article and explore the training ideas included.

For more information about Horizons for Homeless Children
please visit our web site at www.horizonsforhomelesschildren.org or contact Sarah Fujiwara at
sfujiwara@horizonsforhomelesschildren.org or call (617) 287-1900.

CHILD CARE IN UNIQUE ENVIRONMENTS

The Pikler Institute: A Unique Approach to Caring for Children

by Janet Gonzalez-Mena, Elsa Chahin, and Laura Briley

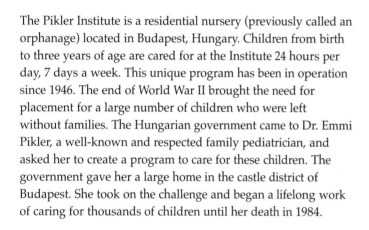

The Pikler Institute is a residential nursery (previously called an orphanage) located in Budapest, Hungary. Children from birth to three years of age are cared for at the Institute 24 hours per day, 7 days a week. This unique program has been in operation since 1946. The end of World War II brought the need for placement for a large number of children who were left without families. The Hungarian government came to Dr. Emmi Pikler, a well-known and respected family pediatrician, and asked her to create a program to care for these children. The government gave her a large home in the castle district of Budapest. She took on the challenge and began a lifelong work of caring for thousands of children until her death in 1984.

This Institute and the research that was Pikler's hallmark continues today under the directorship of Anna Tardos, a psychologist and Emmi Pikler's daughter. Also continuing is the training for professionals and, of course, the care for the children, who are no longer war orphans, but can be thought of as *social orphans*. Their parents are still alive, but the children have been abandoned or their families cannot provide for them. The Pikler Institute is a universal model and has shown that children who live in institutions can grow up to be successful, productive adults.

Elements of the Pikler Approach

Three main elements make up the Pikler Approach: freedom of movement, free play, and caregiving routines. So what makes the Pikler Approach different from other approaches? A beginning of an answer is that the Pikler Approach includes intensive training and support for the nurses, an emphasis on observation, record-keeping and research, and specific ways in which each of these elements are carried out.

Freedom of movement

We'll start with what is probably the most unusual feature of the approach — freedom of movement. Freedom of movement is a cornerstone of the successful, long-term outcomes of the Pikler children, as documented by the World Health Organization. Freedom of movement means that the children are never put in positions that they can't get into by themselves. They are never propped in a sitting position or held in a standing one. They aren't placed in restrictive devices such as infant seats, high chairs, jumpers, or walkers. They lie on their backs, awake or asleep, until they are able to roll over by themselves. The rule is: no adult interference with children's movement.

Emmi Pikler thoroughly researched the concept of freedom of movement in the 1930s with the families for whom she was a pediatrician. When she founded the Pikler Institute, she trained caregivers (called nurses, though they do not have a medical background) to not interrupt the child's freedom of movement. She continued to research the child's development — research that is still going on today.

Allowing children to move freely in their infancy results in remarkably competent balance, coordination, and calculated risk-taking. Anyone who has seen children in the Pikler Institute — whether in person or on video — is impressed by the ease and confidence with which they move their bodies. Old black and white movies from the Pikler Institute show toddlers descending steep stone steps with all the confidence in the world. They know how to handle their bodies, they have impressive equilibrium, and their body awareness is far above average. The Institute has an extremely low accident rate.

Sixty years ago, no one was talking about "Back to Sleep," but Pikler was doing it — back-to-sleep and back-to-play as well.

It's notable that there has never been a SIDS incident at the Pikler Institute. Nowadays babies in the United States are mostly put to sleep on their backs, and as a result there's a strong push to teach parents and caregivers to turn children over when they're awake. Advocates for "tummy time" issue dire warnings about compromised development and misshapen heads. Interesting that neither of these problems are seen at the Pikler Institute, though the babies are never on their tummies until they can turn over by themselves.

Freedom of movement not only results in outstanding gross motor development, but also a strong sense of competence within each baby who finds out that he can learn on his own and doesn't need an adult. Emotional security and self-confidence are the result. When you observe, you can see how lively, exploratory, and, in many ways, self-sufficient the children are, even as infants. They get along with each other remarkably well also.

Free play

Freedom of movement also facilitates the development of fine motor skills. At the Pikler Institute, babies have been closely observed for the last 60 years. As a result, a great deal of thought has gone into the simple play materials they are offered, playthings that respond to just what the children need at each stage. Because babies are on their backs, they have full use of their hands and arms and can freely explore all that they encounter. The first play materials are simple cotton scarves that babies can pick up, hold, wave, and manipulate. The scarves are introduced at two months of age; before this age, their own hands captivate their curiosity and represent their first experience of discovery.

Instead of toys dangling over children's faces or mobiles hanging above them, children have a variety of appropriate objects that they can grasp, hold, turn, mouth, bang, and drop. Just looking at brightly colored objects and trying to bat them is a limited experience and creates frustration. It's much more interesting to manipulate an object — turning it to see all sides. This is how they learn all its properties.

A child who comes from a difficult situation can find calmness in an object that is predictable. As the child plays he is able to believe in the consistency of the objects, when he learns that a cube is always a cube. According to Dr. Gabriella Puspoky, a pediatrician at the Pikler Institute, children can get through a crisis if they have someone to hold on to, as well as objects and self-initiated activities that interest them.

Self-initiated is a key word used at the Pikler Institute. Adults don't entertain or stimulate children. The babies learn to entertain and stimulate themselves, by exploring what their bodies can do, by exploring other babies around them, and by exploring objects and the environment itself. This is quite different from the usual group care situation where someone decides a fussy baby is bored and takes on the job of providing a little entertainment or stimulation — either with a toy or with some kind of activity. The babies at Pikler have plenty of activities, but most of them they invent themselves with the materials available to them.

The reason for minimal adult interaction during free play, according to Anna Tardos, is because the interaction of the adult during the play would never have the same continuity; this impedes predictability. This is why the other cornerstone of the Pikler approach is attentive, present one-on-one caregiving where emphasis is put on predictability. Children not only feel secure when they can predict what will happen, but they come to anticipate the nurse's next move and can thus cooperate with it. Caregiving routines done in this particular way are what allow the child to develop a healthy self-esteem. She knows what will be happening; she has a sense of order in her life.

Caregiving routines

Freedom of movement and self-initiated activities could not be possible if it were not for the all important caregiving routines performed by the child's nurse, who is well trained to carry them out in specific and effective ways. Strong relationships are built with the child and his nurse which leads to trust. Children learn that their needs will be met, even if they have to wait while the caregiver is with another child. They know that when their turn comes the nurse will give careful personal attention and take care of each one of them without haste.

A primary caregiving system insures that each child has a particularly close relationship with one caregiver, though the other caregivers are also important to individuals and to the group. Pikler's idea was to focus the adult/child interactions on the times when the children had to be dependent on the adult and to build a sense of trust that gave them the security to get along without adults at other times — times when they were free to explore and interact with materials and each other. Freedom of movement and uninterrupted play go hand in hand with the focused attention and warm interactions during caregiving times. You can't have one without the other.

Caregiver training

So how does all this happen? How can a balance be created so that the child is free to move and develop at his own rhythm while at the same time be taken care of with much detail? The key is in the care and attention given to training the caregivers. Among other things the caregivers' training includes learning:

■ That each child needs continuous care with an adult in a way that gives consistent personal care. This means that the caregivers stay with the same group of children over time.

■ To see children as competent according to their stage of development. The nurses never ask the children to do more than what they can already do.

■ To give simple choices from a young age. For example, a caregiver shows an 8 month old two pajamas and waits to see which one he points to.

■ To touch children gently. The nurse's kind and gentle touch tells the child she is important and secure. These hands then become something to hang on to and can affect a child positively.

■ To allow each child to fully experience self-initiated activities that he or she enjoys.

■ To allow children to play uninterrupted. The nurses are available should the child need them. Children are never made to feel abandoned. If a caregiver in a particular moment could not tend to one child because she is bathing, feeding, or diapering another, she will assure with her gentle tone of voice that she hears him, and will be with him as soon as she is done.

Caregivers are given the training and then they make it their own, resulting in authenticity. Their feelings toward the children are genuine, and a healthy attachment grows as the adult and child become partners. The quality of the relationship has been carefully designed so that the attachment is secure, but not so strong that the children can't leave their nurses to be adopted or to return to their birth families. The idea is to give children a special kind of relationship at the Pikler Institute that allows them to easily form an attachment in their new or original family with the adult now caring for them. Their brain has been wired to trust; they have come to trust themselves. And this is the best gift a child can give himself.

For more information, contact the Pikler/Loczy Fund USA www.pikler.org.

A Study Course was held in Budapest, Hungary, June 12-23, 2006. For more information inquire at pikler-tardos@axelero.hu or write to the Pikler Institute, Loczy Lajos u.3, H-1022 Budapest, Hungary.

Janet Gonzalez-Mena is on the faculty of WestEd's Program for Infant-Toddler (PITC) Training of Trainer Institutes. She is co-author of *Infants, Toddlers, and Caregivers* and wrote *Dragon Mom*. Janet has an MA from Pacific Oaks College, was a student of Magda Gerber, and has been learning about the Pikler Approach since 2003.

Elsa Chahin was born in México and grew up in both the United States and México. She is an infant-toddler expert specializing in the Pikler approach and travels internationally to train professionals in the field of Early Childhood on how to care for young children with respect.

Laura Briley is President/Owner of Day Schools, Inc. She has been in the early childhood field since 1976. She currently operates four NAEYC-accredited Child Development Centers in Tulsa, Oklahoma. She worked in Romania from 1990-1995 setting up a preschool at Orphange #5 and a kindergarten in a state-run program in Bucharest. Laura is Founder and President of the Pikler/Loczy Fund USA, of which Janet and Elsa are board members. All three authors have observed at the Pikler Institute as well as attending multiple trainings there. They were responsible for organizing a recent study tour to Budapest for 60 participants to study the Pikler Approach.

Using Beginnings Workshop to Train Teachers by Kay Albrecht

Consider the possibilities: Explore ways to apply the concept of freedom of movement in infant and toddler classrooms.

Self-initiation resources: Take a field trip to an infant or toddler classroom and sort toys and materials into two groups — self-initiated or adult-initiated. Remove the adult-initiated ones and observe to see what happens. Ask teachers to reflect on the experience and share their experiences in a newsletter article for infant and toddler families.

Another advocate for primary teaching: Although long recommended as a crucial feature of high quality programs, primary teaching is not as prevalent in U.S. programs as it is elsewhere in the world. Convene staff to discuss and consider strategies for adding this important feature to your program.